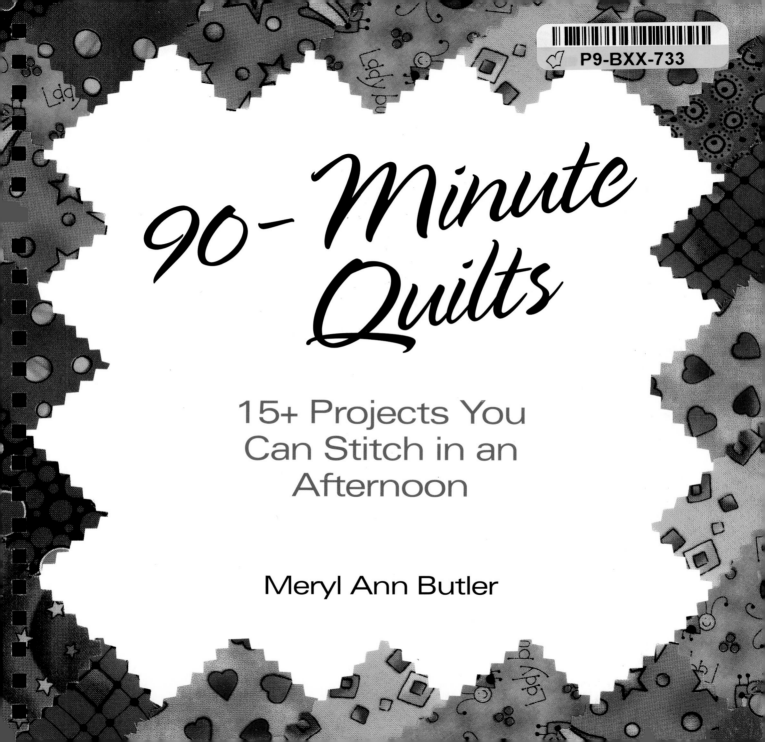

90-Minute Quilts

15+ Projects You Can Stitch in an Afternoon

Meryl Ann Butler

©2006 by Meryl Ann Butler
Published by

kp krause publications
An Imprint of F+W Publications

700 East State Street • Iola, WI 54990-0001
715-445-2214 • 888-457-2873

The following trademarked terms and companies appear in this publication:
505® Spray and Fix, Aleene's® Original Tacky Glue, Benartex, Boston Revolver,
Cherrywood Fabrics, Clover, Coats & Clark, EZ Glitzer®, Flaneltik®, Free Spirit, GlowLine™ Tape,
Heirloom® Organic, Hobbs, IDT®, InvisiGrip™, Isacord , Machine 60/40 Blend®,
Michael Miller Fabrics, Micron®, Moutain Mist®, National Nonwovens, OLFA®, Omnigrid®, P&B Textiles,
Pfaff®, Polarfleece®, Princess Mirah Designs, QuiltCare® Liquid Wash, RJR Fabrics, Robert Kaufman
Fabrics, Schmetz, Soft & Black®, Sharpie®, Soft & Bright®, Springs Creative Products Goup, Sterlite,
Teflon®, Thai Silks, Thermore®, Timeless Treasures, VIP Select®, Warm & Natural®, Warm & White®,
Warm™ Company, Weeks Dye Works™

Library of Congress Catalog Number: 2006922397

ISBN-13: 978-0-89689-325-2
ISBN-10: 0-89689-325-1

Edited by Tracy L. Conradt and Maria L. Turner
Designed by Kara Grundman and Marilyn McGrane

Printed in China

Dedication

To Mom...
who always told me I should be writing; this is for you.

I will always treasure the moment I found out that this book proposal had been accepted, and how that news brought sunny smiles and congratulations from you, even through the fogs of dementia and painkillers. It was a magical moment I will always remember.

Mom, this dedication comes laced with deep appreciation for showing us all how to walk through the door to the life beyond this one with extraordinary grace.

Also dedicated to:
- my amazing daughter, Angelica, with love; I am proud of you and grateful to be your mom.
- the nursing staff on 5 South at the Berkshire Medical Center with deep appreciation.
- my seven creative and talented stepchildren: Randy, Kevin, Stacy, Jennifer, Alison, Galen and Justin.
- the grandchildren already here and those yet to be.

I am so thankful to participate in weaving the threads of the cycles of life with my family, my loved ones and my students.

Acknowledgments

With thanks and appreciation to:
- My editors Maria Turner and Tracy Conradt, illustrator Jana Tappa and designers Kara Grundman and Marilyn McGrane, and all the others at Krause Publications who worked on the publishing aspects of this book.
- Susan Deal, who did the embroidery for the machine embroidered heirloom baby quilt and contributed the embroidery instructions to that chapter. Her friendship and assistance have been indispensible to the completion of this book.
- Andie Schlueter, who made the Dogs and Bones wall hanging.
- Rali Burleson, Susan Deal, Chandler Fox, Trish Schmeidl and Maria Turner for contributing quilts to the Gallery, page 148.
- Bobbie Suratt and Charlene Eschbach for test-driving the instructions.
- Nate Arceneaux, Ralph H. Butler, Aaron Perry, C. Angelica Perry, Garrett Perry, Hanah Perry, Mia Perry and Trent Perry for loaning quilts from their collections.
- Joy Quinn Blum, Wendy Christine Duke, Norma Eckroate, Marsha Moldenhauer, Kathy Ruyts, Triskana West and Cheryl Trostrud-White, whose friendship and kind assistance contributed directly and indirectly to the successful completion of this book.
- All the companies, listed in the Resources, page 159, for providing their great products.

Table of Contents

The Dawn of Remembrance: Egyptian Mysteries *Unveiled*. Fairfield Fashion Show, 1998/99. *Meryl Ann Butler*. Staff by Wendy Christine Duke *(formerly Wendy Bush Hackney)*, Headpiece by Wendy Christine Duke and Meryl Ann Butler.

Gypsy Starcatcher Dancing the Dreams. Fairfield Fashion Show, 1996/97. *Meryl Ann Butler*.

Jewels of India. Bernina Fashion Show, 2005/06 - *Inspiration*. Meryl Ann Butler.

Introduction

When life is so hectic that six minutes feels like too much time to invest in microwaving dinner, few of us can find the leisure time for quilting that our grandmothers enjoyed. Yet, we still have the same heartfelt desires to make quilts for our loved ones and for community service projects. But how can we ever stitch enough quilts for everyone? Adopting clever timesaving techniques makes it possible!

Being a mom of eight motivated me to develop fast methods so that my limited time for quilting would be as fun and effective as possible. I developed the beginnings of my 90-Minute Quilts techniques in 1984 in order to teach my 7-year-old how to make her first quilt, which she delightedly exhibited in my guild's annual show. Today, I'm thrilled to use these speedy techniques to make 90-Minute Quilts for my grandbabies. These cheerful little quilts are fun, fast and washable. And if they get stained or worn out, I just stitch up a replacement in an hour and a half!

Quilters familiar with my complex fiber art over the last couple of decades have been surprised to find me dancing at the other end of the spectrum. And yet, viewed from the perspective of balance, it doesn't seem so odd. After spending months on a fashion show ensemble or commissioned fiber art with thousands of pieces, taking a day off to complete a few 90-Minute Quilts can be very satisfying, allowing me to return to my main project with renewed enthusiasm. In fact, while many beginning quilters love my 90-Minute Quilts classes, experienced quilters do, too. Haunted by their UFOs under the bed, they are thrilled to find a project they can finish in a flash!

And in these uncertain times, people are turning toward the reassurances of the homespun crafts from their childhood memories. Both making and receiving quilts contribute toward soothing concerns about an ever-changing world. After all, quilts aren't called "comforters" for nothing!

Now everyone who thought they didn't have time for quilting can feel a sense of accomplishment, enthusiasm and creativity while stitching up a houseful of happy 90-Minute Quilts.

Have fun!

Meryl Ann

Getting Started

THE basic 90-Minute Quilt can be pieced, quilted and bound in about 90 minutes once you master the timesaving method. Some of the techniques that make the *90-Minute Quilts* process so fast are possible because of the innovations on the sewing machine itself, such as the needle down function, the even feed or walking foot, and the knee lever. If you have these functions on your machine, it will contribute to your speed and efficiency. If not, you will still be able to make a quilt in record time! And the fabulous new quilting tools—from notions like magnetic pincushions and removable tape for marking your ruler, to equipment like the revolving cutting mat to the innovative uses of rotary cutting tools—all assist in speeding up the process. We may have less time to quilt than Grandma had, but we can make up for that with timesaving techniques and devices!

90-Minute Timesaving Tools

The tools and notions showcased in this chapter will help you become efficient with such quilting basics as cutting and pressing. If you are already a quilter, you likely have most of these items on hand. If you are new to quilting, however, you will want to start collecting the basics of mats, rulers, rotary cutters and pins, and then invest in additional tools as you go.

CUTTING TOOLS

Cutting out the fabric blocks is the first step in creating all of the 90-Minute Quilts. The following tools will help you save time.

MATS

For most projects in this book, a rotary mat at least 18" x 24" is required; larger sizes such as 24" x 30" are even better.

ROTARY CUTTERS

Rotary cutters are available in a variety of shapes and sizes. Size 60 mm or 45 mm cutters with ergonomic handles are recommended.

Save your old rotary cutter for blades that have gotten too dull for cutting fabric, but are still sharp enough to cut paper and template material.

RULERS

Clear plastic non-slip rulers are essential for accurate cutting. Ruler sizes used for most of the projects in this book are the 6" x 24" and 6" square. A 120"-long tape is useful for measuring larger quilts.

TRANSPARENT FLUORESCENT TAPE

Tape that temporarily adheres to the ruler to highlight selected cutting lines makes it easier to relocate lines on the ruler in repetitive cutting.

SCISSORS & THREAD SNIPS

Cushioned, nonslip Omnigrid scissors are lightweight and comfortable to use. Keep a pair of thread snips or scissors by the machine to clip threads quickly as you sew.

VIEWING WINDOW

Cut a 5½" square window in a piece of cardboard for viewing the finished size of motifs that will be fussy-cut.

Position a cardboard window over a motif on the fabric to see how the finished square will look.

NOTIONS

Various other notions will help you on your way to your 90-minute quilting success.

PINS AND PINCUSHIONS

Magnetic and wrist pincushions save time in the pinning process. Flat flower-head quilting pins won't unbalance a ruler placed on top of them for rotary cutting. Curved safety pins for quilting are good for kids to use since the sharp pin point is not exposed.

CHALK AND MARKING PENS

Powdered chalk markers have refills and are an effective way to temporarily mark your project.

Permanent markers are useful for making templates, coloring over thread mistakes and marking fabric within seam allowances.

NEEDLE THREADERS

Standard and deluxe needle threaders make threading machine- or hand-sewing needles fast and easy.

SEAM RIPPER, HEM GAUGE AND BODKINS

A seam ripper, hem gauge and bodkins for pulling ribbon through casings are other small tools that come in handy while quilting. Squizzors make remaining unwanted stitches easy and almost fun.

SPRAY ADHESIVE

A temporary fabric adhesive is essential for embroidered quilt projects. I recommend 505 Spray and Fix. It is "the only adhesive spray found not to yellow fabric."

Chalk markers come in several colors.

PRESSING HELPERS

A lightweight mini-iron is an easy way to press seams and can be a safer iron for young sewers to use.

A synthetic velvet pressing board protects the pile when pressing velvet or corduroy, and the Teflon iron sheet protects the iron and board when fusing interfacing.

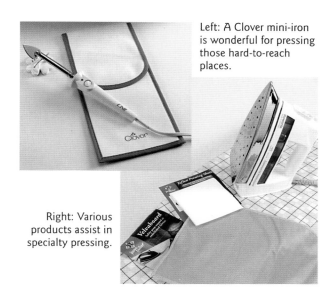

Left: A Clover mini-iron is wonderful for pressing those hard-to-reach places.

Right: Various products assist in specialty pressing.

STORAGE AND CARE

Store extra 6" squares in plastic or archival cardboard boxes large enough for the squares to lie flat, such as the #1695 Sterlite Mini Crate plastic tote.

I recommend QuiltCare Liquid Wash as an excellent laundering product for quilting fabrics. It is also great for natural fiber clothing, lingerie and linens. It is "earth friendly," contains no phosphates or bleach and is bio-degradable.

For long-term storage, wrap the quilt first with archival quality, acid-free tissue paper and store in archival bags or boxes.

FABRICS, BATTING AND THREAD

To ensure timesaving success in creating the projects

Fairfield's storage bag and the archival quality, acid-free tissue paper make it easy to present and store an heirloom baby quilt, protected for generations to come.

in this book, here are the best options in fabrics, batting and thread, as detailed in the following sections.

FABRICS

Fabrics of 100-percent cotton are used in all of the projects in this book, except those that specify another fiber, such as silk or velvet. The substantially sized 6" blocks can showcase an exciting motif. These quilts also are a great way to use up a stash!

Recommended backing fabrics for the projects in this book include flannel, Polarfleece, microfiber plush, silk noil and silk duppioni. In most of the projects in this book, the self-binding is the same fabric as the backing, usually flannel. Flannel is user-friendly, since it tends to stay where it's put, often without pinning. This speeds up the quilt-making process.

Since the backing flannel is visible on the front of the 90-Minute Quilt, its color and design should coordinate with the other fabrics used in the quilt. Overall prints or mottled effects are good choices for backing/binding flannels. Stripes, plaids, nap or one-way designs are not suitable, because when the backing flips to the front to become a self-binding, a nap or one-way design can look crooked or uneven.

• A flannel sheet can be used as a seamless backing for larger quilts. For best results, select 100-percent cotton.
• Fat quarters are rarely cut wide enough to utilize the full 18" width of the fabric, so there is a lot of waste when using them for 90-Minute Quilts. The exception is fat quarters of hand-dyed fabrics, which are usually cut more generously.
• A long quarter of fabric (9") will yield six 6" squares; 3/8 yd, which is just a few more inches of fabric (13½") will yield twice as many squares. If the fabric is over 42" wide, you'll get another "bonus" square across the width.

SELECTING FABRIC COLORS

The study of color can be a pursuit for an entire book—or a lifetime! It's a good idea to become familiar with the basic color wheel with primary, secondary and tertiary colors. There are a couple of tricks that can help anyone select colors more effectively.

COORDINATE VS. MATCHING

Choosing fabrics to coordinate is not the same as matching colors. Usually, the best coordinates are fabrics with less intensity than the focus fabric. The most frequent color mistake that quilters make is judging how fabrics interact with each other from too close a perspective. We typically look at fabric on the bolt at a much closer range than when we view a finished quilt, and this distorts color perception.

To get a better idea of how your selected fabrics will look when they have been combined in a quilt, arrange bolts or swatches so that you can see a larger amount of the fabrics that will be more predominant in your quilt, and less of the fabrics that will be accents. Stand back a few feet, squint your eyes and you will have a better idea of how the group will work together.

PREWASHING FABRIC

Prewashing and drying all fabric is recommended. It preshrinks the fabric, removes chemical sizing and is a good way to find out if any fabric dyes will run when washed before you invest in making your quilt.

Flannel and silk noil often shrink significantly, so it is imperative to prewash them. Silk noil may need to be prewashed twice, as it may continue to shrink the second time it is washed and dried.

When machine-washing small pieces of fabric (fat quarters, long quarters or smaller pieces) place them into a zippered lingerie bag and wash on the gentle cycle to prevent tangling and excessive unraveling.

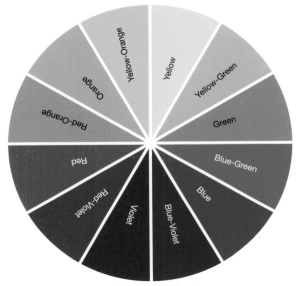

A basic color wheel.

BATTING

Battings come in a wide variety of colors, weights and styles. Choose a batting that can be quilted up to 6"-7" apart for most of the projects in this book. Check batting packaging or contact the manufacturer for this information, or select your batting from the list that follows.

Choose battings with a very flexible drape for doll quilts and stiffer, denser battings for wall hangings. Cotton flannel fabric can also be used in place of batting, especially when the backing is made of a silk noil or cotton.

Loft is the height of the batting, usually from ⅛" to ¾" high or more. Higher loft makes a bulkier quilt and tends to be very forgiving, hiding seams that don't match perfectly in its depth!

The thinnest batting is recommended for larger quilts, since it adds less bulk to the mass of the quilt sandwich you need to negotiate through the space under the arm of the machine. It is also the best choice for enhancing the drapability of doll quilts.

Fleece batting (not to be confused with Polarfleece) is a denser batt recommended for extra firmness in wall hangings and gameboards.

Polyester offers more loft and washability, while natural fibers such as cotton, wool/cashmere or silk have a cozier feel. Blends offer a bit of both.

Batting comes in a variety of colors. Refer to projects for suggestions.

The following battings have been used in the projects in this book:
- Machine 60/40 Blend Batting (Fairfield)
- Thermore Ultra Thin Batting, Heirloom Organic (Hobbs)
- White Rose & Cream Rose, A Touch of Silk, A Touch of Cashmere (Mountain Mist)
- Warm & Natural, Warm & White, Soft and Bright, Warm Fleece, Soft and Black and Warm Blend (Warm Company)
- Matilda's Own Wool Batt (in Australia see Victorian Textiles; in North America see Quilter's Resource)

THREAD

Don't skimp on thread! Use good-quality, brand-name cotton, polyester or cotton-covered polyester thread. Cheap threads may save a few pennies at the register, but their fragile fibers fill your machine with debris, making machine servicing necessary more often.

A great spacesaver for your sewing room: store batting overhead in an inexpensive, lightweight hammock! Select a location, remembering that it will sag much lower when it is filled with batting. Install two hooks in your ceiling or near the top of two walls from which to suspend it. (I used the hooks for hanging planters. Select the appropriate size for the amount of weight that you expect to be supporting.) Hang the hammock rings on the hooks and pop your batting in. It's easy to see what you have, and it puts unused space to work.

90-Minute Timesaving Techniques

You will be referring to these sections for all projects in the book. For easy reference, mark these pages with paper clips, postable notes or adhesive page dividers.

PRESSING VS. IRONING

Ironing is a side-to-side movement that can stretch delicate fabric. Pressing is an up-and-down motion: picking up the iron, setting it down on the fabric and lifting it again. The projects in this book instruct you to press the fabrics to avoid stretching the fabric which could result in difficulty in the final quilt construction.

ROTARY CUTTING SQUARES

You will need a rotary cutter, a cutting mat at least 18" x 24" and a 6" x 24" ruler. Use GlowLine tape or small postable notes to highlight the cutting line on the ruler. Trim the selvages off the fabric, as they may shrink more with every washing.

Fussy-cutting is required when a specific motif in the fabric needs to be framed in a square. Use the markings on a 6" square ruler to line up the center of the motif, and rotary cut for a perfect fussy-cut square. More yardage is required for fussy-cut motifs. The exact amount depends on the size of the motifs and the length of the repeat.

LAYING OUT SQUARES

Arrange squares out on a flat design surface, such as cutting board or flannel board, following the Quilt Layout for each project. Pin a postable note on each square On the top row, numbering left to right, label the columns.

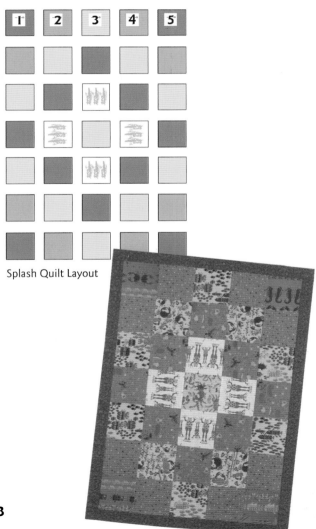

Splash Quilt Layout

SEWING THE SQUARES

1. Stack up the squares in each column, being careful to keep them in order.

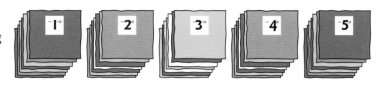

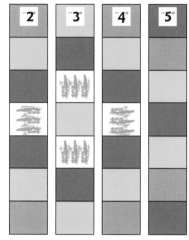

2. Use a walking foot with ¼" marking, quilting foot or other foot with a ¼" seam allowance to stitch together the squares in column 1, being careful to keep them in order. Cotton squares tend to adhere to each other and a walking foot or even-feed will keep the fabric from slipping, so experienced sewers may not need to pin the squares together. If you do use pins, be sure to either remove them as you sew, or position pins out of range of the needle. Leave the postable note with the column number pinned to the top square.

3. Repeat step 2 for remaining columns and then place each sewn strip back onto the design surface in the appropriate position, checking to make sure each square is sewn in the proper place.

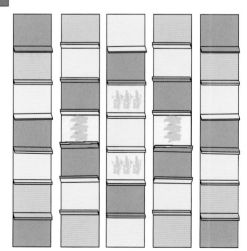

4. Press the seam allowances down, away from the top square, on odd-numbered columns. Press the seam allowances up, toward the top square, on even-numbered columns.

ADDING THE BACKING

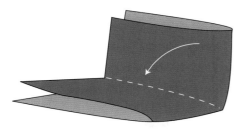

1. With wrong sides together, press the flannel backing fabric. Fold it in half, long sides together, and then in half again.

2. Press lightly over corner folds to indicate the approximate center of the backing.

3. Open and place the backing right-side down on a flat surface, smoothing out the wrinkles.

4. Determine if your quilt will contain batting. If using batting, go to the Adding the Batting section (page 16). If not using batting, go to the Sewing the Columns section (page 17).

BACKINGS FOR LARGER QUILTS

For larger quilts, either use a flannel sheet for backing or stitch yardage together as follows.

1. Place flannel backing right sides together.

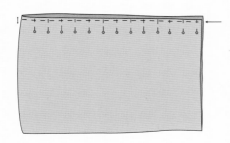

2. Pin and stitch with seam allowance ⅝" from selvage.

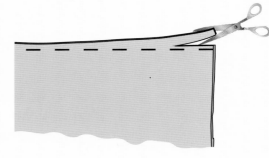

3. Trim ⅜" off selvages.

4. Press seam allowance open. Continue to stitch fabric pieces together to obtain desired size of backing fabric.

ADDING THE BATTING

1. Fold the batting in half and in half again.

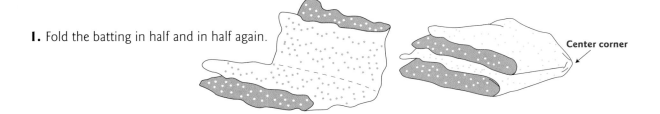

Center corner

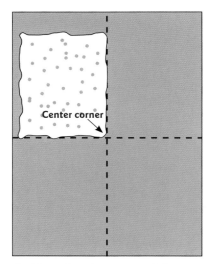

Center corner

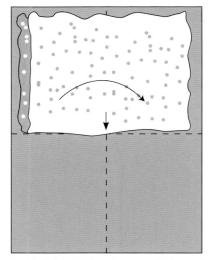

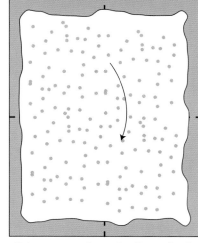

2. Note the placement of the center of the flannel backing marked by pressing and line up the inside corner of the folded batting with this center point.

3. Unfold the batting carefully and it will be centered on the flannel. The batting and the flannel backing will not be exactly the same size, which is normal at this stage.

SEWING THE COLUMNS

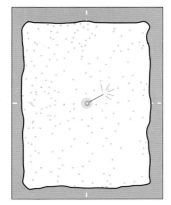

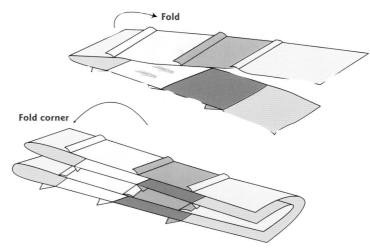

1. Carefully lift up one corner of the flannel and stick a long pin through the center marking, straight up from the bottom, through the flannel (and through the batting, if you are using it). You should see the pin sticking up on the top side.

2. Pick up the center column. (This is column 3 in a quilt with five columns, column 4 in a quilt with seven columns, and column 5 in a quilt with nine columns.) Find the center of this column by folding it in half lengthwise, with right sides together, and then folding it in half again crosswise.

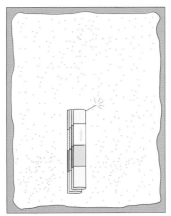

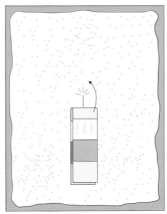

3. Line up the folded corner with the pin that is sticking up.

4. Unfold the column and remove pin.

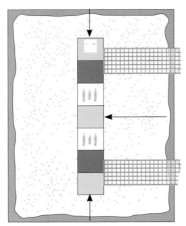

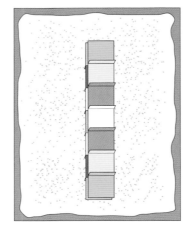

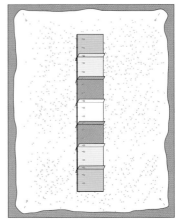

5. Measure as shown to make sure the column is accurately centered on the batting/backing unit. Also, measure the distances at the top and bottom edges of the column to the backing batting unit.

6. Place the adjacent column with the next lower number over the center column, right sides together. In this example, column 2 is placed over column 3.

7. Pin along the left raw edge, fitting seam allowances into each other like puzzle pieces, pinning through visible seam allowances.

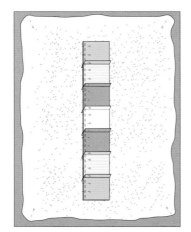

8. Insert bobbin thread to match backing fabric. Use an even feed foot or engage the even feed function, increase the stitch length slightly and stitch columns together (unless otherwise instructed) backstitching at the beginning and end of the seam.

9. Check the stitching on the back of the quilt to make sure there are no unwanted tucks.

 Slightly pulling the top portion of the quilt sandwich away from the needle as you sew can help avoid pleats.

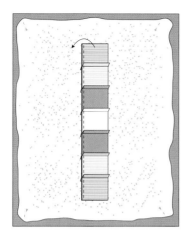

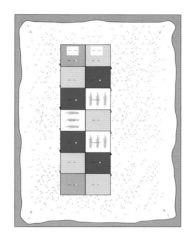

Especially for larger size quilts, roll sides of quilt in, then fold accordion-style in your lap for easier handling when stitching.

10. Unpin and flip the stitched column open, smoothing it out. Press lightly if desired.

11. Check the stitching on the front to make sure the seam was stitched appropriately, with no raw edges peeking through. Then pin this column down flat through batting and backing.

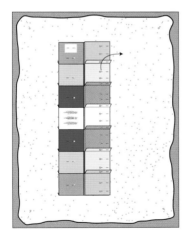

12. Repeat steps 6 through 11 with next adjacent, larger-numbered column. In this example, it is column 4

13. Repeat steps 6 through 12 with remaining columns in order.

QUILTING THE PROJECT

1. Remove the pinned papers with the column numbers on them and discard.

2. Smooth out and pin the corners and raw edges down with straight pins or quilters' safety pins.

3. Thread the machine with thread that contrasts with the top and load the bobbin with thread to match the backing. Start with a full bobbin.

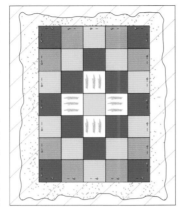

5. Stitch to ¼" of raw edges on outside squares. When you get to a stopping point at the edge of the squares, leave the needle in the down position, raise the presser foot and reposition the quilt, lower presser foot, and begin stitching along the next diagonal.

6. Backstitch when you have finished the first pass, which is when you arrive at the corner that is diagonally opposite from where you started.

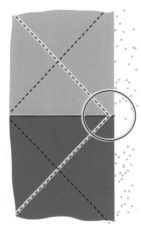

4. Begin in a corner by first backstitching and then machine quilting a straight line across each square from corner to corner of each square on the diagonal.

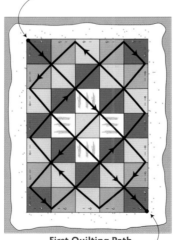

First Quilting Path

7. Begin the second pass at either remaining empty corner and continue as in steps 4 through 6. Remove the pins.

Second Quilting Path

ADDING BORDERS

Some of the quilts in this book have borders. To create these borders, complete the steps that follow. For projects without borders, skip this section and go to Self-Binding on page 23.

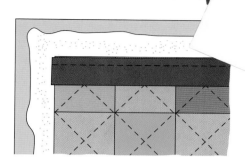

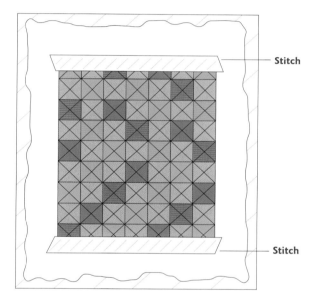

1. Cut border fabric into strips as directed in project instructions. For larger sizes, you may need to piece pairs of border strips to create longer strips.

2. Pin borders, with right sides together, to top and bottom, matching raw edges. Extend border strips at least ¼" beyond raw edges to allow for shifting of fabric when stitching. Trim ½" beyond raw edge.

3. Stitch border strips with ¼" seam allowance to top and bottom of pieced quilt top, backstitching at the beginning and end of the seam. (In some instances, directions may have you add borders to the sides first.)

4. Flip border strips open and press. Border may extend about ¼" past the edge of the quilted squares. Trim slightly, if desired, but not much! It's better to have a little excess fabric than not enough.

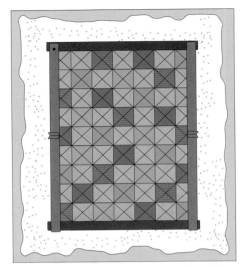

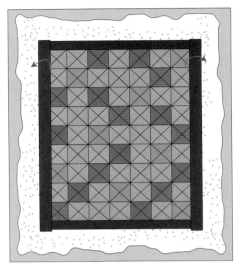

5. Pin two longer border strips, right sides together, along the raw edges of each long side of the pieced quilt top and stitch.

7. Flip side border strips open and press. Border will extend about ¼" past edge of quilted squares. Trim slightly, if desired.

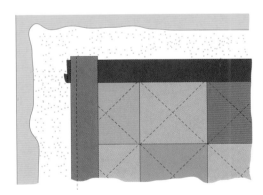

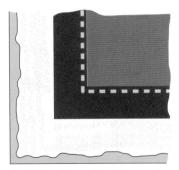

6. Trim, allowing border strip to extend about ¼" from edge.

8. Optional: Add a line of quilting stitches on the inside of the border, using the presser foot as a width guide. Start partway down one side, not in the corners. Backstitch at beginning and end of stitching. Use the needle-down function to pivot at corners and, if available, markings on presser foot to assist in gauging where to end stitching lines at corners.

SELF-BINDING

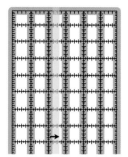

1. Place transparent fluorescent tape or two or three small postable notes along the 3½" measuring line of your 6" x 24" ruler to ensure accuracy in measuring. If desired, draw arrows, as shown, to indicate measuring line selected.

3. Repeat step 2 on bottom of the quilt, followed by each of the two sides.

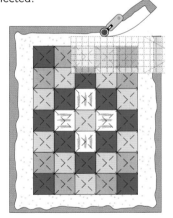

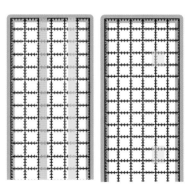

2. Start at the top of the quilt and rotary cut the backing fabric the specified amount, usually 3½" from the raw edge of pieced squares. You will be cutting through some of the batting, too.

4. Place a different color of transparent fluorescent tape or two or three small postable notes along the 1¼" measuring line of your ruler for accuracy in cutting. (I keep a 6" x 24" ruler permanently marked with the transparent fluorescent tape on the 3½" and 1¼" lines to use with all my 90-Minute Quilt projects.) If desired, add arrows as in step 1.

5. Fold the top backing flap back, right sides together, making sure the backing is folded securely away from the batting.

6. Trim the <u>batting only</u> the specified amount, usually 1¼" from the raw edge of the pieced squares being sure that the backing is folded securely away from the batting.

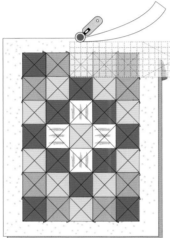

7. Flip the backing fabric back up.

8. Repeat steps 5, 6 and 7 on the bottom of the quilt, followed by each of the sides.

9. Press in the raw edge of the backing, wrong sides together, a generous ¼" to ⅜" on both long sides. Note: Before pressing, fold the raw edge to determine which measurement works best for your quilt. Variation is due to thickness of batting selected, as well as variations in stitching. However, when you determine the exact width for your quilt, use that same measurement all around the quilt. This fold will need to cover a generous ¼" - ⅜" of the raw edge of the pieced blocks.

Stitching the top after stitching the sides forms a self-casing for hanging the quilt if desired. If you wish to hang your quilt horizontally, stitch top and bottom first, followed by the long sides. If you don't plan to hang your quilt, and you prefer a more finished edge, leave the thread tails from the machine stitching on the quilt, thread a needle with one or both of them and blindstitch the openings shut.

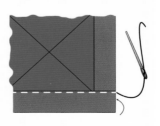

10. Fold the flannel backing over the batting and pin in place, making sure that the flannel covers a generous ¼" - ⅜" of the raw edge of the pieced blocks.

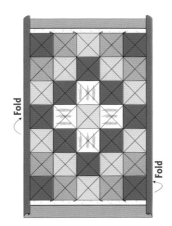

11. Use a seam guide to make sure the self binding is even. The actual measurement may vary slightly based on the thickness of the batting.

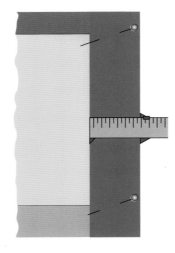

In step 12, if you notice that some raw edges did escape being covered with binding, there's no need to rip out the whole seam. Just "unsew" 2" to 3" on either side of the offending area, re-pin, being sure to overlap the raw edges sufficiently, and re-sew.

12. Edgestitch with thread to match backing/binding, beginning at edges of the backing. Edgestitching is topstitching that is stitched very close to the edge of the fabric, within ¹⁄₁₆". Check edgestitched areas closely to make sure that the raw edges of blocks underneath were caught in the stitches.

13. Repeat step 9 on the top and bottom, except that after pressing under raw edges, open them and fold corner in to make neat corners.

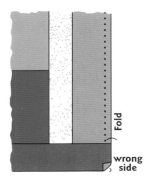

14. Repeat steps 10 through 12 on the top and bottom.

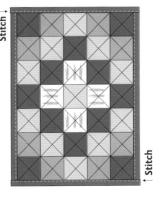

MAKING BIAS BINDING
(ALTERNATE BINDING TECHNIQUE)

Bias binding takes longer to make than self-binding, but there are times you may want to use it, such as for a more finished look on an elegant quilt or heirloom quilt. For a decorative effect, use a fabric for the binding that is different from the backing.

I. Lay out fabric on cutting mat, line up 45-degree angle of ruler with lower selvage and rotary cut.

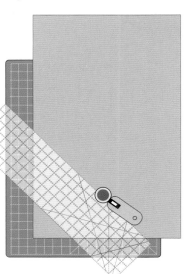

2. Fold fabric, right sides together. Depending on the size of your cutting mat, fabric may need to be repositioned one or more times.

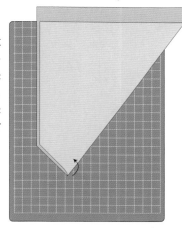

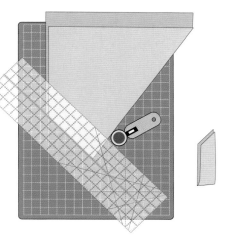

3. Mark 2⅝" line of ruler with transparent fluorescent tape or postable notes. Line up the 2⅝" line with the bias-cut raw edge of fabric and rotary cut a strip. Cut additional bias strips 2⅝" wide. Trim any selvages. Place strips around the edge of the unfinished quilt so you can tell when you have cut enough strips, allowing extra for seams.

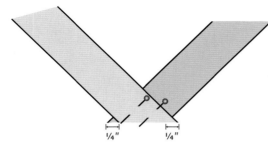

4. Pin bias strips, right sides together, with triangles hanging out at each side.

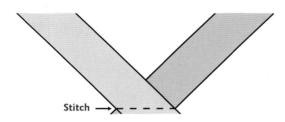

5. Stitch all seams together with ¼" seam allowance. Make sure seams are all on the same side of the bias strip. Trim seam to ¼".

6. Gently press seams open along grainline to prevent stretching bias.

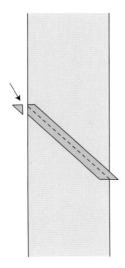

7. Trim overhang.

 Store stitched binding rolled around discarded toilet paper or paper towel tube.

ATTACHING BIAS BINDING

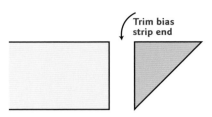

1. Trim one end of bias strip.

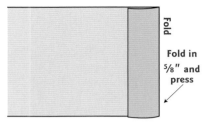

2. Fold end in ⅝", wrong sides together, and press.

3. Pin bias binding to edge of quilt, right sides together, pinning on fold as shown at right. Begin partway on one side, not a corner.

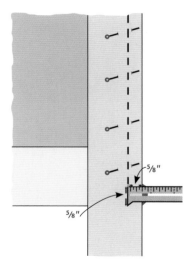

4. Using a seam gauge to measure, mark a dot ⅝" in from corner.

5. Stitch a ⅝" seam allowance to dot. Remove pins.

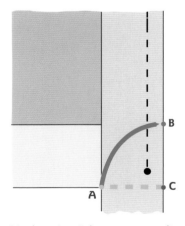

6. Pinch point A between two fingers, lift and bring to point B, holding down at point C and folding up along dotted line.

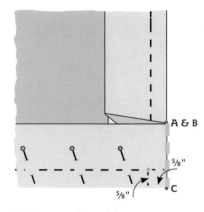

7. Pin, mark and begin sewing at dot.

8. Continue as in steps 3 through 8 on all four sides.

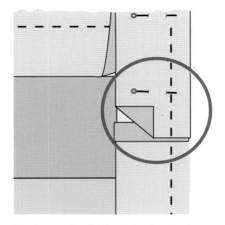

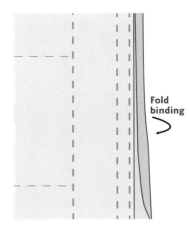

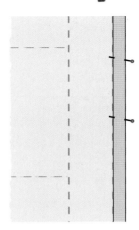

9. Cover the fold of the beginning of the binding strip up to the raw edge and trim. Pin and stitch.

10. Remove all pins and fold binding in half, wrong sides together.

11. On one side, fold binding again to cover the ⅝" stitching line and pin.

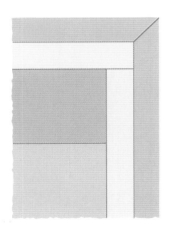

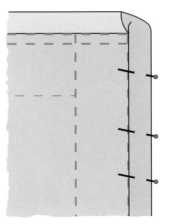

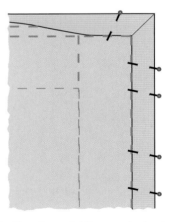

12. Open binding at corners and fold back.

13. Continue folding binding under on next side and pinning to cover the ⅝" stitching line.

14. Continue folding and pinning binding on remaining sides.

15. Hand-stitch binding to finish.

CREATING FOUR-PATCH DESIGNS

ASSEMBLE THE TOP

Use four squares, 6" x 6" from the border and backing fabrics. All seam allowances are ¼".

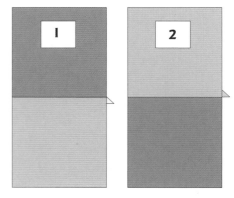

1. Sew 6" squares, right sides together, to form two two-square "columns".

2. Label left hand column 1 and right hand column 2.

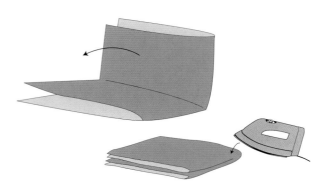

3. Press seams down in column 1 and up in column 2.

4. Fold flannel backing in half and in half again and press to mark center.

5. Open and place the flannel backing right-side down on a flat surface, smoothing out wrinkles.

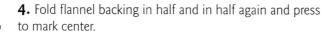

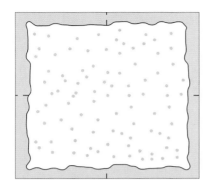

6. Layer the batting centered on top of the flannel backing.

7. Carefully lift up one corner of the flannel and stick a long pin through the center marking, straight up from the bottom, through the flannel and the batting. You should see the pin sticking up through the batting. Pin the four corners of batting with regular pins or quilting pins.

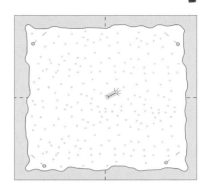

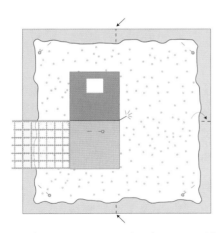

8. Line up the center seam of column 1 with the protruding pin. Measure, as shown, to make sure the raw edges of column 1 are parallel to the edges of the backing fabric.

9. Place column 2 over column 1, right sides together, and pin along the center raw edge through all layers, fitting seam allowances into each other like puzzle pieces.

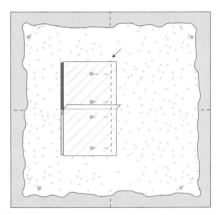

10. Stitch column 1 to column 2 along pinned raw edge, through batting and backing, using a walking foot if available with a ¼" seam allowance. Slightly stretching the quilt sandwich as you sew can help avoid pleats.

11. Remove pins, open column 2 and remove and discard the pinned papers with column numbers. Press lightly if desired.

QUILT THE TOP

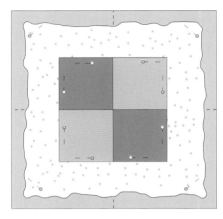

1. Pin the corners and raw edges down with straight pins or quilters' curved safety pins.

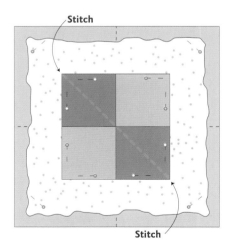

2. Start in any corner and using contrasting thread, backstitch and then machine quilt a straight line across from corner to corner, backstitching again at end of seam.

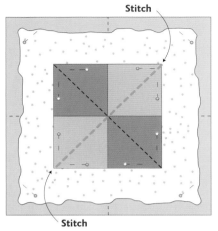

3. Repeat with other corners.

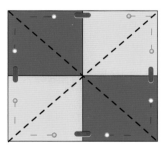

4. Measure in ¼" from raw edge of four seams and mark.

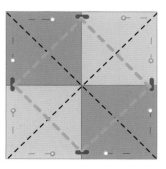

5. Stitch this square. When you get to a corner, leave the needle in the down position, raise the presser foot, reposition the project and lower the presser foot to begin stitching along the next diagonal.

ADD THE BORDER

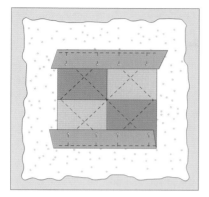

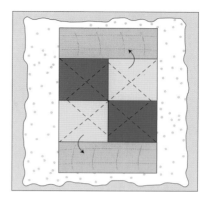

1. Stitch border strips around the edges, log cabin style, beginning by pinning and stitching the top and bottom strips.

2. Fold open and press open the top and bottom border strips.

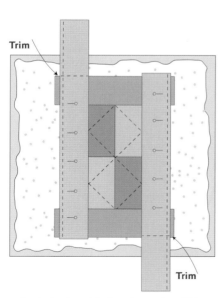

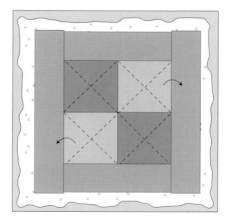

3. Pin and stitch the side border strips. Trim.

4. Fold open and press open the side border strips.

5. Self-bind, as detailed for the full-size quilts, page 23.

Author, Meryl Ann Butler, works with student, Chandler Fox, as she stitches her own 90-Minute Quilt. Photo by Photographs by Susie.

Sewing with Kids

Sharing sewing with kids can start them out on a lifelong love of sewing and creativity. Three of the most important things to keep in mind are: selecting manageable projects, creating a learning-supportive environment with effective tools and equipment, and providing a lot of positive reinforcement.

PROJECT PREPARATION

Select a quick-and-easy project for the initial sewing experience, such as the It's In the Bag project, Dogs and Bones wall hanging, My Dolly's Quilt or a four-patch pillow cover. These can be finished in just one or two short sewing sessions.

Encourage kids to choose their own fabrics and colors.

Gentle guidance toward considering fabrics with motifs of their favorite things like horses, ballerinas, race cars or sports can be useful, but kids will be more enthusiastic about the project if the final choice is left up to them. It's helpful to bring a 5½" viewing window to the fabric store with you.

KID-FRIENDLY TOOLS

I prefer to teach kids on a sewing machine with a walking foot attachment. The foot is user-friendly, helping to avoid lumps and bumps, and its bulk helps keep fingers away from the moving needle. I generally have my young students use the width of the walking foot for their seam allowance. This is usually a bit larger than ¼", so the finished item may come out slightly smaller, but that is not an issue for any of the projects in this book.

It's important to select lightweight age- and size-appropriate scissors.

I mark seam allowances with a chalk marker for beginning students. It is easier for them to follow a line at first, like having training wheels on a bike.

Initially, I pin the critical areas for them, such as ends and middle of seams, and I let them place the remaining pins in-between.

For beginning projects, I often rotary cut some of the 6" squares for them. I let them cut their own fussy-cut squares using the 6" square ruler and marking with chalk before cutting out with scissors. I never let youngsters use a rotary cutter.

KID-FRIENDLY TECHNIQUES

For ease in organizing, group project pieces in zipper-style plastic gallon and two-gallon bags, and corral everything in a big plastic container with a lid. Let the child label the bag with the title of the contents, such as "Leftover Fabric and Scraps," "Cut Squares," etc.

HAVE FUN

The most important aspect of sewing for kids is to enjoy the process together. First projects set the tone for young ones' relationships to sewing and quilting for the rest of their lives. Twenty years later, these children will not remember how long it took to make their projects, but they will remember if they had fun.

PRAISE OFTEN

Building self-esteem enhances all areas of life at home, in school and in social activities. For my own eight kids, I made it a point to display their artistic, sewing and craft projects prominently in our home. Nothing says "I'm proud of you" as loudly as a parent's actions.

Inviting youngsters to enter their sewn and quilted items in the county fair or other nonjuried exhibition encourages a sense of pride in completing a project. Winning a prize is nice, if it happens, but displaying the work is the main event. Taking a photo of the child next to her displayed work is another way to build positive self-image and keep the momentum of interest going for more sewing projects.

BE PATIENT

It will take kids quite a bit longer than 90 minutes to make any of the projects in this book because they will not be using some of the timesaving tools (such as a rotary cutter) and techniques. Nevertheless, this is the fastest type of quilt they can make, and they will have a sense of great accomplishment with a relatively minimal investment of time and effort.

TIMESAVING TECHNIQUES

Timesaving techniques include:

• Use of the presser foot knee lift, if your machine has one.

• Engaging the needle-down function, especially when pivoting.

• Pincushions (both standard and magnetic) save time by keeping the pins handy.

Troubleshooting Q & A

There are no "mistakes"—only educational opportunities. Some projects may have a different direction in mind than what you thought when you started. It's usually less stressful and a lot more fun to go with the flow than to fight it!

Q Oops! After I started my first line of stitching, I realized I had the wrong color in the bobbin. Now what?

A If the color of backing fabric is darker than the bobbin thread, you can color it in with Micron pen or Sharpie marker.

How to prevent this next time: Do all piecing and stitching with the backing color thread in the bobbin.

Q My backing is too short to make self-binding. How do I bind my quilt now?

A Trim the batting shorter than the prescribed amount, so the backing has less batting to fold over. Or, trim the backing flush with the batting and add bias binding.

How to prevent this next time: Cut the backing larger or measure more accurately when placing the center column.

Q My thread broke in the middle of a long line of quilting. How do I continue?

A Pull threads to the back of the quilt and tie a double knot. With a needle threader, thread a long (3" is great) large-eyed needle such as those used in dollmaking. Pull the needle through the quilt <u>between</u> the front and back, pulling the needle as far as possible before pulling it up on the back side of the quilt. Shorter threads will be buried inside the quilt. Longer threads can be trimmed off.

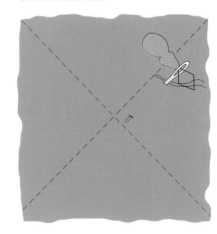

36

Q I'm making a quilt larger than the table surface I have to work on and it's difficult to pin it. What do you suggest?

A Consider buying a piece of foam core board larger than your tabletop. (Larger sizes are available in framing/art stores.) The foam core board can be stored flat against the wall behind a large piece of furniture such as buffet, headboard or bureau when not in use. Cover one side with flannel for an instant design board.

Q Oh no! I didn't fold my backing over far enough, and I sliced through it while rotary cutting the batting!

Is my quilt ruined?

A No, you can heal the wound with iron-on interfacing and some zigzag stitching in a color to match the backing fabric. Or add bias binding as detailed earlier.

How to prevent this next time: Fold backing over very carefully, pinning if it doesn't want to stick to itself or if it is not flannel.

Q Oops! I finished my whole quilt and then I noticed a spot on the front where my seam allowance wasn't large enough, and now the batting is sticking out of the little hole in my quilt. Now what?

A This is a great opportunity for an appliqué, either one you make from coordinating fabrics or a purchased, iron-on one.

How to prevent this next time: Check each seam carefully after every step.

Q My quilt is done and a pin is sewn inside it! Do I have to take the whole quilt apart to get it out?

A Luckily, no you don't. Find the closest seam, carefully remove a few stitches and pull the pin out (tweezers can help). Close the opening using a blindstitch. If it's a wall hanging, and the pin inside has a glass head, protect the project on the top and bottom of the area where the pin is with heavy cardboard. With a hammer, hit the pinhead. A glass head will shatter, and you can pull the pin out. Because this leaves little pieces of glass inside, this is appropriate for wall hangings, but not for quilts that will be washed and cuddled.

Q Big disaster! Any solutions?

A Time to think outside the box! Cut up your quilt into a wearable. It's already lined; just add bias binding to the raw edges or serge.

Designing Your Own Layouts

Photocopy the design templates provided and use colored pencils or fabric swatches and glue stick for planning your design.

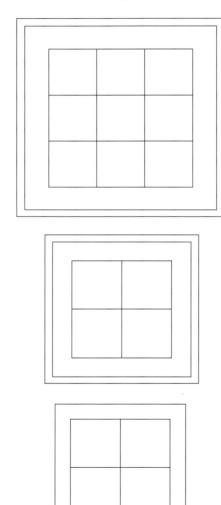

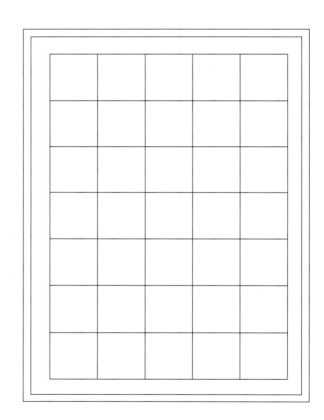

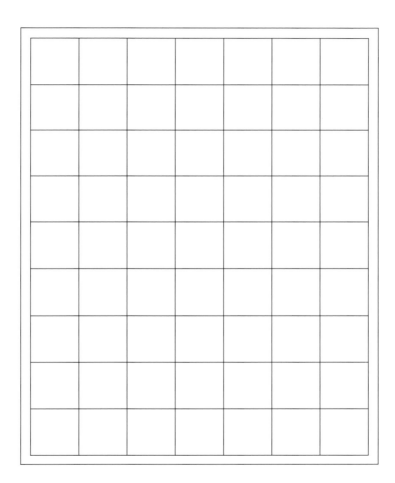

Projects

ENJOY learning the timesaving 90-minute quilting methods with these fast and fun projects. From basic crib-size quilts to pillows, doll quilts, throw-size quilts, wall hangings, game board quilts and a shawl.

Don't expect to finish your very first (or even your second) 90-Minute Quilt in an hour and a half, since you will be taking time to learn and perfect new techniques. Once you master the 90-minute methods, you'll be able to make the basic crib-size quilt projects in about 90 minutes of actual sewing and construction time; the larger "snuggle" or throw-size quilts will take longer to make simply because they are bigger. Even so, these are some of the "fastest quilts in the west!" If you want especially fast results, try a small project, such as a wall hanging, a pillow or the Tic-Tac-Toe game quilt.

Basic Trip Around the World

Once you become familiar with the clever, timesaving techniques detailed in Chapter 1, you can stitch a basic baby quilt in 90 minutes! This includes piecing, quilting and binding. What a great bazaar item.

Finished size: 30" x 41"
(5 x 7 squares)

YOU WILL NEED

Enough yardage to fussy-cut selected motif from red fabric (center block)

¼ yd. lime green ladybug fabric (blocks)*

⅜ yd. yellow multicolor dot fabric (blocks)*

⅜ yd. royal blue butterfly fabric (blocks)*

¼ yd. each two "twin" orange print fabrics or substitute ⅜ yd. of one orange print fabric (blocks)

¼ yd. turquoise star fabric (blocks)

1⅜ yd. yellow multicolor dot cotton flannel (binding/backing)*

36" x 48" batting*

Thread to match backing (bobbin)

Additional threads to match other fabrics (piecing blocks)

Contrast thread (top quilting)

Rotary cutter

24" or longer cutting mat

6" x 24" ruler

Several small postable notes

6" square ruler (if fussy cutting)

Transparent fluorescent tape (optional)

*Used in this project: Animal Tales yellow fabric by RJR (blocks); Splish Splash Dots flannel by Robert Kaufman (backing); and Machine 60/40 Blend by Fairfield (batting); Nature's Play green ladybug and royal butterfly fabrics by K.P. Kids & Co. by V.I.P. Select by Cranston.

CUT

1. One square, 6" x 6", fussy-cut from red motif fabric for the center.

2. Cut the following:

- 4 squares, 6" x 6", green ladybug fabric
- 8 squares, 6" x 6", yellow dot fabric
- 10 squares, 6" x 6", royal blue butterfly fabric
- 4 squares, 6" x 6", orange twin fabric 1
- 4 squares, 6" x 6", orange twin fabric 2
- 4 squares, 6" x 6", turquoise star fabric

Note: If you are creating a design significantly different than the one shown in the model, you might begin by cutting 10 squares from each of the six fabrics selected, saving the leftovers for another 90-minute quilt, and moving to step 2 in the Design section that follows.

BEFORE BEGINNING Consult the Getting Started section for piecing, sewing and quilting techniques.

LAYOUT

1. Arrange all squares on a flat designing surface, following the Quilt Layout on page 45 to achieve the same look. Or, if you would like to try creating your own design, continue to How to Create Your Own Design.

SEW

1. Label and sew the squares into columns.

2. Place backing on a flat surface, right-side down, smoothing out any wrinkles and place batting on top.

3. Pin the center column 3 and sew all the columns down.

QUILT

Quilt, using thread to match the backing fabric in the bobbin.

Detail of center square after quilting.

BIND

Trim the backing to 3½" and the batting to 1¼". Follow the Self-Binding section on page 23.

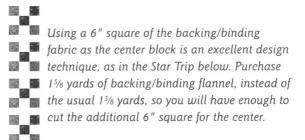

Using a 6" square of the backing/binding fabric as the center block is an excellent design technique, as in the Star Trip below. Purchase 1⅝ yards of backing/binding flannel, instead of the usual 1⅜ yards, so you will have enough to cut the additional 6" square for the center.

Star Trip

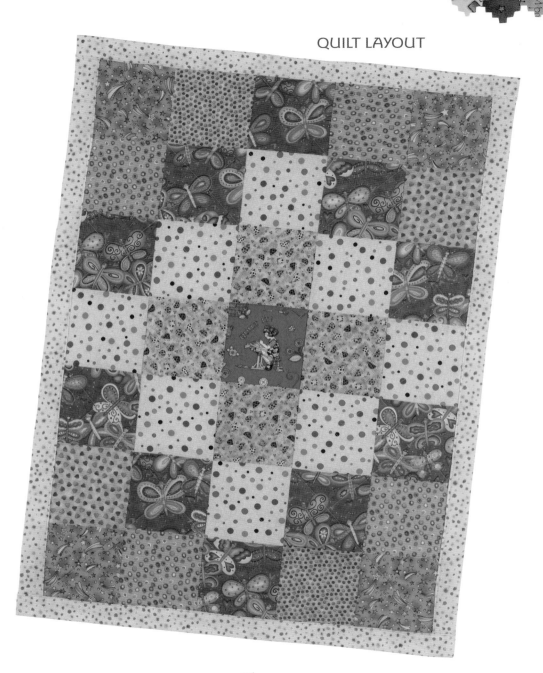

HOW TO CREATE YOUR OWN DESIGN

1. Select a 6" square for the center and place the square on the center of the designing surface.

2. Select a contrasting fabric for the four squares around the center square.

An easy way to design a basic Trip Around the World Quilt is to use the same predominant color for the center square as is used in the binding/backing, as in Orange Trip (page 47). The center square could be a favorite fabric with a special motif, such as a flower or animal, or simply a bright color that matches or closely coordinates with your backing fabric.

3. Select a fabric for the next group of eight squares.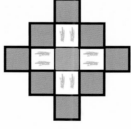

4. Continue with the next group of 10 squares. Twin lime green fabrics were used in the model.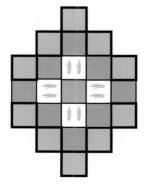

5. Continue with the next group of eight squares. Medium blue dots were used in the model.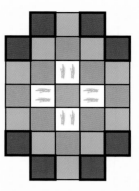

6. Finish with the four corners.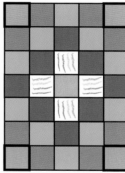

7. Place binding/backing fabric near edge of the design to see how it interacts with the colors around the perimeter. If you like the arrangement, you are finished creating your design. If not, reposition squares as desired until you are pleased with the look.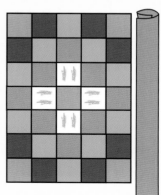

8. To complete the quilt, continue with the Sew, Quilt and Bind steps.

WHAT IS A TWIN FABRIC?

Design interest can be enhanced by substituting a twin fabric in a design, as in the orange blocks in Basic Trip Around the World. These two different but compatible fabrics "read" as the same fabric on first glance. But on closer inspection, you can see that one of these orange fabrics has a heart pattern and the other has a dot pattern. Using twin fabrics retains design integrity in the overall effect of the quilt, but the subtle differences offer textural interest and sparkle. It is also a great solution when you have run out of a fabric!

Orange Trip

47

Streak of Lightning

A single block oriented in different directions creates an exciting complex design!

Finished size: 30" x 41"
(5 x 7 squares)

YOU WILL NEED

1⅜ to 2 yd. (or more; exact amount depends on design repeat) multicolor striped diagonally printed fabric (blocks)*

1⅜ yd. 42"/44"-wide lavender silk noil (backing/binding)*

1¼ yd. flannel (batting)

Thread to match backing (bobbin)

Neutral thread (piecing blocks)

Contrast thread (top quilting)*

Rotary cutter

24" or longer cutting mat

6" x 24" ruler with diagonal lines

6" square ruler

Several small postable notes

Transparent fluorescent tape (optional)

Rotating cutting mat or 12" x 18" cutting mat (optional)

*Used in this project: Multicolor diagonal stripe by Springs (blocks); noil by Thai Silks (backing/binding); and Isacord thread (top quilting).

PREPARE

Fabric selection is the foundation for a great looking Streak of Lightning design. Look for:

- Stripes printed on the diagonal. This is not a bias-cut of fabric.
- Stripes that offer design interest in each 6" square.
- Stripes with a slightly blended or fuzzy edge, rather than sharp or hard edged stripes. Indistinct edges are much more forgiving to work with since they don't need to match up perfectly.

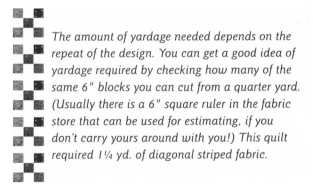

The amount of yardage needed depends on the repeat of the design. You can get a good idea of yardage required by checking how many of the same 6" blocks you can cut from a quarter yard. (Usually there is a 6" square ruler in the fabric store that can be used for estimating, if you don't carry yours around with you!) This quilt required 1¼ yd. of diagonal striped fabric.

BEFORE BEGINNING Consult the Getting Started section for piecing, sewing and quilting techniques.

CUT

1. Select a stripe to be the primary diagonal that will run from corner to corner on your 6" block. You may select any stripe for this, but once you have chosen one, then every 6" square must be cut exactly the same way. (On this fabric, I selected the fuchsia-colored stripe for my primary diagonal.)

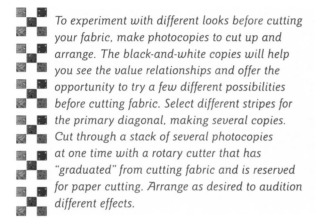 *To experiment with different looks before cutting your fabric, make photocopies to cut up and arrange. The black-and-white copies will help you see the value relationships and offer the opportunity to try a few different possibilities before cutting fabric. Select different stripes for the primary diagonal, making several copies. Cut through a stack of several photocopies at one time with a rotary cutter that has "graduated" from cutting fabric and is reserved for paper cutting. Arrange as desired to audition different effects.*

2. Line up the 45-degree diagonal line of 6" square ruler with the stripe selected. Be aware of the colors of the triangle shapes created by cutting the stripes at the two other corners. These will help you line up the ruler the same every time.

3. Cut 35 total 6" squares exactly the same (aligning the same stripe with the 45-degree line).

4. Trim silk noil backing to 38" x 49".

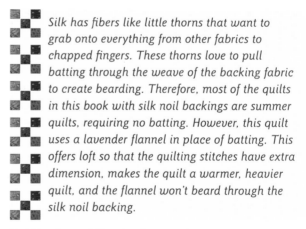 *Silk has fibers like little thorns that want to grab onto everything from other fabrics to chapped fingers. These thorns love to pull batting through the weave of the backing fabric to create bearding. Therefore, most of the quilts in this book with silk noil backings are summer quilts, requiring no batting. However, this quilt uses a lavender flannel in place of batting. This offers loft so that the quilting stitches have extra dimension, makes the quilt a warmer, heavier quilt, and the flannel won't beard through the silk noil backing.*

5. Trim flannel "batting" to 36" x 48".

LAYOUT

Arrange all the squares, following the Quilt Layout for the same look shown.

 Even after the 6" squares are cut, there are many design placement possibilities with this technique. Rearranging the squares into a variety of exciting designs is one of the most enjoyable parts of making a Streak of Lightning quilt! Be creative!

SEW

1. Label and sew the squares into columns.

2. Place silk noil backing on a flat surface, right-side down, smoothing out any wrinkles, and then place flannel "batting" on top.

3. Pin the center column 3 and sew all columns down.

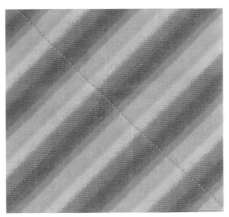

Detail of center square after quilting.

QUILT

Quilt, using thread to match the backing fabric in the bobbin. On this quilt, the first pass of stitching was done with fuchsia thread. The second pass was done with green thread.

BIND

Trim the backing to 3½" and the batting to 1¼". Follow the Self-Binding section on page 23.

QUILT LAYOUT

51

Bright Basketweave

With *clever cutting and positioning, just one brightly colored striped fabric creates a bold, bright, basketweave effect.*

Finished size: 30" x 41"
(5 x 7 squares)

YOU WILL NEED

1⅜ yd. (or more; exact amount depends on design repeat) primary colored striped fabric (blocks)*

36" x 48" batting*

1⅜ yd. flannel (backing)*

Thread to match backing (bobbin)

Neutral thread (piecing blocks)

Contrast thread (top quilting and edgestitching)

Rotary cutter

24" or longer cutting mat

6" x 24" ruler

6" square ruler

Several small postable notes

Transparent fluorescent tape (optional)

*Used in this project: Flannel by Robert Kaufman (backing) and Mountain Mist White Rose (batting).

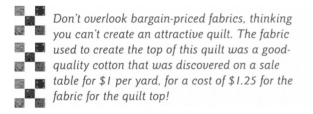

Don't overlook bargain-priced fabrics, thinking you can't create an attractive quilt. The fabric used to create the top of this quilt was a good-quality cotton that was discovered on a sale table for $1 per yard, for a cost of $1.25 for the fabric for the quilt top!

BEFORE BEGINNING Consult the Getting Started section for piecing, sewing and quilting techniques.

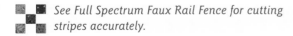

See Full Spectrum Faux Rail Fence for cutting stripes accurately.

CUT

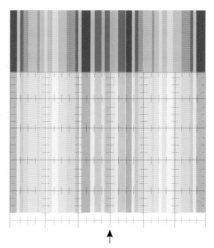

1. Line up the center marking of the 6" square ruler with the selected stripe and cut strips. Then sub-cut (18) 6" squares exactly the same (aligning same stripe with center ruler line for each). These will be the vertical blocks. In this project, the center line of the ruler was lined up with the green stripe.

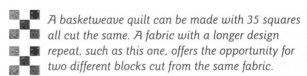

A basketweave quilt can be made with 35 squares all cut the same. A fabric with a longer design repeat, such as this one, offers the opportunity for two different blocks cut from the same fabric.

2. Line up the center marking of the 6" square ruler with another selected stripe on the block fabric and cut (17) 6" squares exactly the same (aligning same stripe with center ruler line for each). These will be the horizontal blocks. In this project, the center line of the ruler was lined up with the yellow stripe.

3. Trim flannel backing to 38" x 49".

LAYOUT

Arrange all the squares, following the Quilt Layout to achieve the same look shown.

SEW

1. Label and sew squares into columns.

2. Place backing on a flat surface, right-side down, smoothing out any wrinkles and place batting on top.

3. Pin the center column 3 and sew all columns down.

QUILT

Quilt, using thread to match the backing fabric in the bobbin.

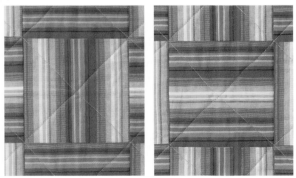

Detail of two squares on the quilt front after quilting.

BIND

Trim the backing to 3½" and batting 1¼". Follow the Self-Binding section on page 23.

QUILT LAYOUT

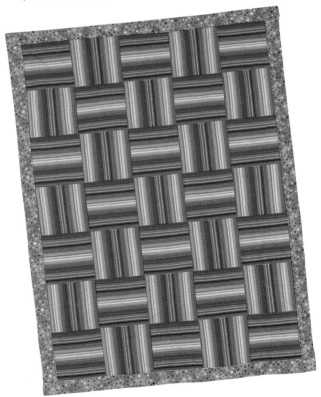

This pretty pastel basketweave is an easier variation of the Bright Basketweave quilt. The blocks didn't need to be fussy-cut because the fabric features a softer, more forgiving linear motif. This version only requires 1 yd. of fabric.
Finished size: 30" x 41" (5 x 7 squares)

Racy
Checkerboard

This easy checkerboard design requires only two contrasting fabrics for the squares.

Finished size: 30″ x 41″
(5 x 7 squares)

YOU WILL NEED

⅝ yd. racecar motif with black background fabric (blocks)

⅝ yd. red dot fabric (blocks)*

1⅜ yd. blue tone-on-tone print cotton flannel (backing)

36" x 48" batting*

Thread to match backing (bobbin)*

Neutral thread (piecing blocks)

Contrast thread (top quilting)*

Rotary cutter

24" or longer cutting mat

6" x 24" ruler

6" square ruler

Several small postable notes

Transparent fluorescent tape (optional)

*Used in this project: Animal Tales by RJR (dot blocks); 60/40 batting by Fairfield; and Isacord thread (top and bobbin).

BEFORE BEGINNING Consult the Getting Started section for piecing, sewing and quilting techniques.

CUT

Note: Individual squares are not cut for this technique.

I. Cut as follows:

- (3) 6" strips, selvage to selvage, racecar fabric

- (3) 6" strips, selvage to selvage, red dot fabric

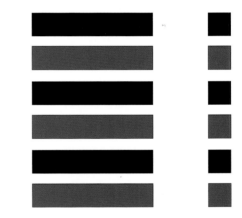

2. Use a 6" square ruler to measure and then cut one 6" square from the end of each strip from step I. Set aside.

SEW

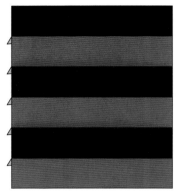

1. Stitch the six alternating fabric strips, right sides together, along the long edges with ¼" seam allowance, creating a stripped unit.

2. Press seams down.

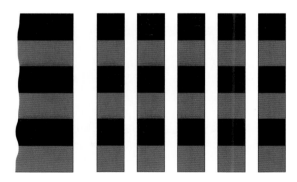

3. Use a 6" x 24" ruler to crosscut five 6"-wide strips from the stripped unit.

4. Label columns 1 through 5, from left to right, with postable notes pinned to each.

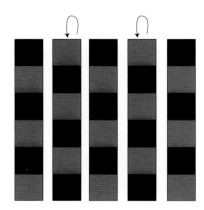

5. Reverse columns 2 and 4 so the bottom square is now at the top, right-side up, creating the checkerboard effect. Re-pin the postable notes to the tops of these two columns.

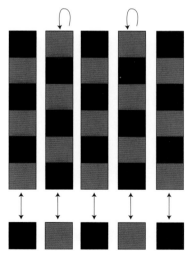

6. Stitch an appropriate 6" square to the bottom of each column so each column is seven squares long.

7. Press seam allowances on the added squares in the same direction as other seam allowances in the same column.

8. Place the backing on a flat surface, right-side down, smoothing out any wrinkles. Place the batting on top.

9. Pin the center column 3 and sew all columns down.

QUILT

Quilt, using thread to match the backing fabric in the bobbin.

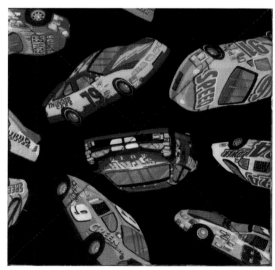

Detail of square on the quilt front after quilting.

BIND

Trim the backing to 3½" and the batting to 1¼". Follow the Self-Binding section on page 23.

QUILT LAYOUT

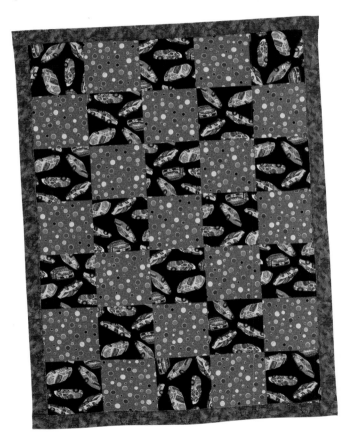

Bali Batik
Baby Quilt

This lovely little quilt is a variation of the basic checkerboard design. Made without batting, it gets its body from the soft flannel backing. It's a perfect lightweight quilt for keeping baby comfortable on cool summer evenings.

Finished size: 30" x 41"
(5 x 7 squares)

YOU WILL NEED

⅝ yd. light batik fabric (blocks)

⅝ yd. dark batik fabric (blocks)

1⅜ yd. teal tone-on-tone print cotton flannel (backing)

Thread to match backing (bobbin)*

Neutral thread (piecing blocks)

Contrast thread (top quilting)*

Rotary cutter

24" or longer cutting mat

6" x 24" ruler

6" square ruler

Several small postable notes

Transparent fluorescent tape (optional)

BEFORE BEGINNING Consult the Getting Started section for piecing, sewing and quilting techniques.

INSTRUCTIONS

1. Choose light batik fabric in pale browns, sienna, teal or lavender and dark batik in darker browns, sienna, teal and purple.

2. Follow instructions from the Racy Checkerboard quilt, page 56, omitting the batting instructions.

QUILT LAYOUT

Faux Rail Fence

Create a rail fence look with the clever use of striped fabric. This all-flannel quilt has soft and cuddly baby appeal.

Finished size: 30" x 41"
(5 x 7 squares)

YOU WILL NEED

⅜ yd. yellow mini-print flannel (blocks)*

⅜ yd. green mini-print flannel (blocks)*

1 yd. (or more; exact amount depends on design repeat) striped fabric*

1⅜ yd. pink mini-print flannel (backing)*

36" x 48" batting*

Thread to match backing (bobbin)

Neutral thread (piecing blocks)

Pink thread (top quilting and edgestitching)

24" or longer cutting mat

6" x 24" ruler

6" square ruler

Several small postable notes

Transparent fluorescent tape (optional)

*Used in this project: Estrella flannels by FreeSpirit and Cream Rose batting by Mountain Mist.

BEFORE BEGINNING Consult the Getting Started section for piecing, sewing and quilting techniques.

CUT

1. Cut, as follows:
   - 9 squares, 6" x 6", yellow mini-print flannel
   - 8 squares, 6" x 6", green mini-print flannel

2. Line up the center marking of the 6" square ruler with selected stripe on block fabric and cut three strips. Aligning the same stripe with center ruler line for each. Then subcut (18) 6" squares exactly the same. Refer to instructions for Bright Basketweave, page 52.

3. Trim flannel backing to 38" x 49".

LAYOUT

Arrange all the squares on a flat designing surface. Follow the Quilt Layout for the same look.

SEW

1. Label and sew squares into columns.

2. Place the backing on a flat surface, right-side down, smoothing out any wrinkles and place batting on top.

3. Pin the center column 3 and sew all columns down.

QUILT

Quilt, using thread to match the backing fabric in the bobbin.

BIND

Trim the backing to 3½" and batting to 1¼". Follow the Self-Binding instructions on page 23.

QUILT LAYOUT

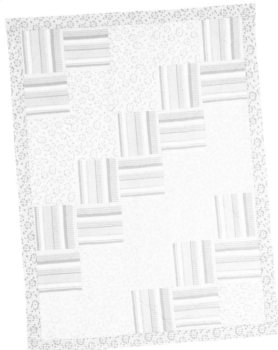

Full Spectrum Faux Rail Fence

This larger snuggle quilt shimmers with the vibrant colors of gradation stripe fabrics. The timesaving methods used in the basic 90-Minute Quilts are an effective way to make bigger quilts, too. You'll be surprised at how quickly you can finish one!

Finished size: 52" x 62"
(9 x 11 squares)

YOU WILL NEED

Note: Yardages listed are for these fabrics only; other similar fabrics may require different yardage amounts, depending on size of stripe and repeat lengths.

1 yd. rose striped fabric (blocks for both light rose and dark rose)*

1¼ yd. tangerine striped fabric (blocks)*

⅞ yd. yellow striped fabric (blocks)*

⅞ yd. lime green striped fabric (blocks)*

⅔ yd. turquoise/green striped fabric (blocks)*

1 yd. deep royal striped fabric (blocks)*

⅝ yd. purple striped fabric (blocks for both light purple and dark purple)*

3⅝ yd. coordinating Bali batik flannel (backing)*

58" x 70" thin batting*

Thread to match backing (bobbin)

Neutral thread (piecing blocks)

Contrast thread (top quilting and edgestitching)

Rotary cutter

24" or longer cutting mat

6" x 24" ruler

6" square ruler

Several small postable notes

Transparent fluorescent tape (optional)

3" x 18" ruler (optional)

*Used in this project: Narrow band Fundamentals gradating stripes by FreeSpirit (blocks); Bali Flanneltik by Princess Mirah Designs (backing); and Thermore Ultra Thin batting by Hobbs.

BEFORE BEGINNING Consult the Getting Started section for piecing, sewing and quilting techniques.

CUT

1. Fussy-cut the darker rose striped fabric by first lining up the selected stripe on a 6" x 24" ruler.

2. Rotary cut around perimeter of ruler, shifting the ruler slightly while cutting so the final piece is 6" x 25". (This extra inch offers a bit of leeway for miscuts.)

3. Subcut 6″ squares by turning 6″ x 24″ fabric strip at 90-degree angle to create four identical fussy-cut squares.

4. Repeat steps I through 3 two more times on darker rose striped fabric. You will have 12 total squares, but only need nine for this project. Store the other three squares for another project.

5. Fussy-cut the remaining fabrics in the same manner as steps I through 3 to obtain the number of squares needed, as follows:
- 3 squares, 6″ x 6″, lighter color stripe of rose-colored fabric
- 13 squares, 6″ x 6″, tangerine striped fabric
- 17 squares, 6″ x 6″, yellow striped fabric
- 18 squares, 6″ x 6″, lime green striped fabric
- 15 squares, 6″ x 6″, turquoise/green striped fabric
- 12 squares, 6″ x 6″, deep royal striped fabric
- 7 squares, 6″ x 6″, lighter purple from purple striped fabric
- 5 squares, 6″ x 6″, darker purple from purple striped fabric

PREPARE BACKING

Create the flannel backing, as detailed on page 15 for Backing For Larger Quilts.

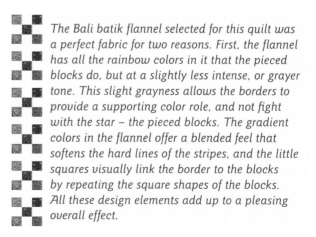

The Bali batik flannel selected for this quilt was a perfect fabric for two reasons. First, the flannel has all the rainbow colors in it that the pieced blocks do, but at a slightly less intense, or grayer tone. This slight grayness allows the borders to provide a supporting color role, and not fight with the star – the pieced blocks. The gradient colors in the flannel offer a blended feel that softens the hard lines of the stripes, and the little squares visually link the border to the blocks by repeating the square shapes of the blocks. All these design elements add up to a pleasing overall effect.

LAYOUT

Arrange all the squares on a flat designing surface to achieve the same look as shown.

SEW

1. Label and sew the squares into columns.

2. Place the backing on a flat surface, right-side down, smoothing out any wrinkles, and place batting on top.

3. Pin the center column 5 and sew all columns down.

QUILT

Quilt, using thread to match the backing fabric in the bobbin.

BIND

1. Trim the backing to 3½" and the batting to 1¼". Follow the Self-Binding instructions on page 23.

 *In this project, the light rose blocks and dark rose blocks are cut from different areas of the same fabric by carefully positioning the ruler to "capture" the group of lighter or darker stripes when cutting the same is true for the light and dark purple stripes. This requires careful planning unless you have unlimited amounts of fabric! To insure accuracy any time you are fussy cutting, it is helpful to mark all planned cuts with chalk before making final cuts.*

Fast, Fun and Funky Flashback

This project is great for encouraging teen and preteen interest in quilting. The funky retro fabrics and glow-in-the-dark thread create a groovy snuggle quilt or wall hanging!

Finished size: 45¼" x 56¼"
(7 x 9 squares plus border)

YOU WILL NEED

⅜ yd. each four colorways tie-dye look fabric (blocks)*

¼ yd. each five retro-look prints on black background fabric (blocks)*

6" square retro-look print on black background fabric (center block)

⅝ yd. black with multicolor mini-dot fabric (borders)*

3⅜ yd. 42"-wide cotton flannel (backing)*

52" x 64" thin batting*

Thread to match backing (bobbin)

Neutral thread (piecing blocks)

Glow-in-the-dark thread (top quilting)*

Rotary cutter

24" or longer cutting mat

6" x 24" ruler

6" square ruler (optional for fussy cutting)

Several small postable notes

Size 90/14 sharp machine needles (optional)*

3"-wide long ruler (optional)

*Used in this project: Caryl Fallert's Aurora Style 126 by Benartex in Emerald, Ultramarine, Amethyst and Rubylite (blocks); Smilie Faces and X-Tremely Hip by V.I.P. by Cranston (blocks); Freckles by FreeSpirit (borders); Fossil Fern Flannel by Benartex #131 Winter Sunset (backing); Thermore by Hobbs (batting); NiteLite ExtraGlow thread by Superior in pink and green (thread); and Microtex Sharp Needles by Schmetz (required due to thickness of NiteLite ExtraGlow thread).

BEFORE BEGINNING Consult the Getting Started section for piecing, sewing and quilting techniques.

CUT

Cut, as follows:

- 8 squares, 6" x 6", from each of the four different tie-dye look fabrics for a total of 32 squares
- 31 squares, 6" x 6", assorted squares from the five retro-look prints
- 6 strips, 3" wide, selvage to selvage, multicolor mini-dot border fabric

When using specialty threads, practice stitching on scrap fabric with batting first, adjusting the tension if needed.

PREPARE BACKING

Prepare the backing as detailed on page 15 for Backing For Larger Quilts.

LAYOUT

Arrange all the squares following the Quilt Layout on page 71 for the same look as shown.

SEW

1. Label and sew the squares into columns.

2. Place the backing on a flat surface, right-side down, smoothing out any wrinkles, and place batting on top.

3. Pin the center column 5 and sew all columns down.

QUILT

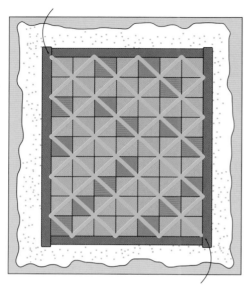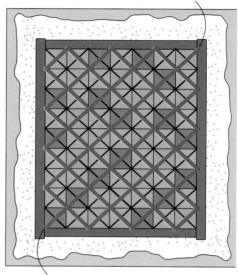

Quilt, using glow-in-the-dark thread on top and thread to match the backing in the bobbin. Some specialty threads are heavier, and the brand you select may require a sharp machine needle with a larger eye. The tension also may need to be adjusted when using different weights for the top and bottom threads. Quilting may be done in all one color, or each pass can be done in a different color, as in this project.

BORDERS

1. Sew together two pairs of 3"-wide selvage to selvage border fabric strips to make two longer strips for the sides.

2. Add borders, following instructions on page 21.

BIND

Trim the backing to 3½" and the batting to 1¼". Follow the Self-Binding instructions on page 23.

Farmers' Market

What a delicious quilt for a kitchen or for your favorite chef! This is a great project for using a fat quarter collection. The summer quilt has no batting.

Finished size: 52" x 64"
(9 x 11 squares)

YOU WILL NEED

21 fat quarters from farmers' market print fabrics or from your favorite collection

1½ yd. dark charcoal with multicolor specks fabric (blocks)

3⅜ yd. mottled rust flannel (backing)*

Thread to match backing (bobbin)

Neutral thread (piecing blocks)

Contrast thread (top quilting)

Rotary cutter

24" or longer cutting mat

6" x 24" ruler

6" square ruler

Several small postable notes

3"-wide long ruler (optional)

*Used in this project: Kyle's Marketplace III (blocks); Confetti Basics (blocks); Crazy for Flannels (backing). All by RJR.

BEFORE BEGINNING Consult the Getting Started section for piecing, sewing and quilting techniques.

CUT

Cut, as follows:
- 50 squares, 6" x 6", charcoal with multi-specks fabric
- 49 squares, 6" x 6", assorted market prints (Although 49 squares are all that are needed, you may consider cutting three squares from each of the 21 prints to allow for design freedom and to leave you with leftover squares for another project!)

LAYOUT

Arrange all the squares following the Quilt Layout on page 75 for the same look as shown. Alternate the food fabrics with the charcoal background fabrics, checkerboard-style. Use a red berries block for the center and place brighter-colored prints toward the center of the quilt, with deeper colors and browner colors toward the outside, for a glowing effect.

SEW

1. Label and sew the squares into columns.

2. Place the backing on a flat surface, right-side down, smoothing out any wrinkles.

3. Pin the center column 5 and sew all columns down.

QUILT

Quilt, using thread to match the backing fabric in the bobbin.

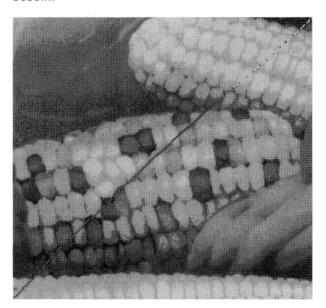

BIND

Trim the backing to 3½". Follow the Self-Binding instructions on page 23.

Detail of binding on one corner of the finished quilt.

Hand-Dyed Gradations Snuggle Quilt

A complex design with an interwoven effect is created by a clever arrangement of color gradations. A cuddly Polarfleece backing fills the dual needs of backing and batting.

Finished size: 46½" x 49½" (8 x 9 squares)

YOU WILL NEED

2 fat quarter sets of 8 hand-dyed gradations fabric in contrasting colors (blocks)*

1¾ yd. 58"-wide coordinating multicolor print Polarfleece (backing)*

Cotton multicolor thread (bobbin and top quilting)*

Neutral thread (piecing blocks)

Rotary cutter

24" or longer cutting mat

6" x 24" ruler

6" square ruler (optional)

Several small postable notes

Transparent fluorescent tape (optional)

3" x 18" ruler (optional)

*Used in this project: Cherrywood suede-look gradations in Alaskan Sunset and Blue Lagoon (blocks); Polarfleece by JoAnns (backing); and Coats & Clark Egyptian Cotton Machine Quilting Thread Size 50 Multicolor #T38 (top and bobbin).

BEFORE BEGINNING Consult the Getting Started section for piecing, sewing and quilting techniques.

CUT

1. Cut Set A fabrics (Blue Lagoon), as follows:
- 1 square, 6" x 6", darkest blue (#1)
- 3 squares, 6" x 6", next darkest blue (#2)
- 5 squares, 6" x 6", next darkest blue (#3)
- 7 squares, 6" x 6", medium dark blue (#4)
- 8 squares, 6" x 6", medium teal (#5)
- 6 squares, 6" x 6", lighter teal (#6)
- 4 squares, 6" x 6", lighter green (#7)
- 2 squares, 6" x 6", lightest yellow-green (#8)

2. Cut Set B fabrics (Alaskan Sunset), as follows:
- 1 square, 6" x 6", darkest purple (#1)
- 3 squares, 6" x 6", next darkest purple (#2)
- 5 squares, 6" x 6", next darkest purple (#3)
- 7 squares, 6" x 6", medium dark plum (#4)
- 8 squares, 6" x 6", medium light fuchsia (#5)
- 6 squares, 6" x 6", dark rose (#6)
- 4 squares, 6" x 6", medium rose (#7)
- 2 squares, 6" x 6", light rose (#8)

LAYOUT

1. Arrange all the Blue Lagoon squares, following the illustration for the same look as shown, beginning with lighter green at upper left and progressing to darker blue at lower right.

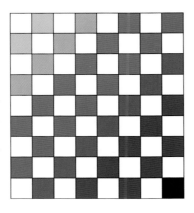

2. Fill in with Alaskan Sunset squares, as shown, referring to the illustration and Quilt Layout on page 79 for the finished look.

If you want to use different eight-step gradations than the ones shown, use the grid paper for an eight square by nine square layout. Glue down fabric swatches or use colored pencils to create your layout. Use the mockup as a cutting and placement guide.

SEW

1. Label and sew the squares into columns.

2. Place the Polarfleece on a flat surface. If your Polarfleece has a right-side, place it right side down.

3. Measure horizontal and vertical center lines of fleece and mark with chalk.

4. Line up and pin the right side of column 4 flush with the vertical center chalk line. (Since this quilt has an even number of columns, there is no center column.)

5. Sew all the columns down.

QUILT

Quilt, using thread to match the backing fabric in the bobbin.

Most hand-dyed fabrics, like these, have no right or wrong side.

DON'T TOSS THE FLEECE!

If there is an 8"- to 12"-wide piece of Polarfleece leftover from your backing, you can make a scarf in a few moments. Here's how:

1. Fold Polarfleece in half, selvage to selvage.

2. Trim both long sides so they are straight and even.

3. Cut decorative-shaped edges using the June Tailor fancy fleece ruler or a wavy-edge rotary blade for fancy edges in a flash!

BIND

Trim the backing to 3½". Following the Self-Binding instructions on page 23.

QUILT LAYOUT

Call of the Wild

This dramatic throw is backed and bound with luxurious microfiber plush. Animal print flannels give the quilt extra body, and the faux fur backing offers loft without batting, so no quilting is needed.

Finished size: 52" x 64"
(9 x 11 squares)

YOU WILL NEED

¼ yd. of 17 different flannel animal print and coordinating fabrics (waleless corduroy or cotton velveteen) or, for a simpler version, ⅜ yd. of nine different fabrics (blocks)

2⅛ yd. 58"-wide black microfiber plush (batting/backing)*

Thread to match backing (bobbin)

Neutral threads (piecing blocks)

Rotary cutter

24" or longer cutting mat

6" x 24" ruler

6" square ruler (optional)

Several small postable notes

Chalk marker

Transparent fluorescent tape (optional)

*Used in this project: black Minkee by Benartex.

BEFORE BEGINNING Consult the Getting Started section for piecing, sewing and quilting techniques.

Select flannel animal print fabrics in a variety of light, medium and dark values, in a range of natural brown tones. Include such designs as cheetah, leopard, tiger, zebra, jaguar and giraffe, as well as mottled duotone flannels in shades of brown. A variety of small, medium and large prints creates textural interest. Two waleless corduroys in light and dark brown provide some solid blocks to balance the busy prints.

CUT

I. Cut 99 total 6" squares from the animal print flannels and waleless corduroy fabrics.

2. Organize blocks in piles of light, medium and dark values.

Select microfiber plush carefully. It should pass the "touch test." Cheaper brands may not feel as luxurious.

LAYOUT

Arrange all the squares following the Quilt Layout on page 83 for the same look as shown. Alternate values and colors to create interest; rotating some of the squares with one-way prints (such as large zebra and tiger prints) or nap, enhances the design.

Take some time when designing the throw top to "play" with the squares to create the most pleasing finished look.

SEW

1. Label and sew the squares into columns.

2. Place microfiber plush backing on a flat surface, right-side down, smoothing out wrinkles.

3. Pin the center column 5 and sew all columns down.

4. Staystitch ¼" in from raw edges of sewn blocks on all four sides.

BIND

1. Trim the backing to 3½" from the raw edge all the way around the pieced top.

2. Use your fingers to roll in the raw edge of the backing ½" on both long sides. Fold it over the pieced squares and pin in place, so the backing covers the staystitching and at least ⅜" of the raw edge of the pieced blocks. Pin generously.

3. Edgestitch each of the sides. Check edgestitched areas closely to make sure fabrics underneath were caught in the stitches.

4. Repeat steps 2 and 3 for the top and bottom of the quilt.

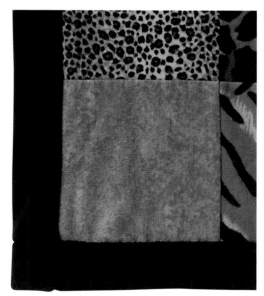

Detail of Minkee microfiber plush corner.

Loving Memories

Old clothing can find new life as a quilt with fond memories in every block! An assortment of receiving blankets, a collection of childhood clothing or a group of T-shirts from a high school or college sports career make memory quilts that are wonderful graduation gifts. This snuggle quilt was made from my mother's clothing as a special way for my daughter to remember her grandmother.

Finished size: 45" x 58"
(7 x 9 squares plus borders)

YOU WILL NEED

Collection of old clothing filled with memories (blocks)

Purchased coordinating fabrics (blocks)* (optional)

⅝ yd. purchased coordinating fabric (border)

Fusible interfacing (weight and amount determined by clothing selected)

1¾ yd. 60"-wide microfiber plush, or Polarfleece/flannel sheet and batting of choice (backing/batting)*

Thread to match backing (bobbin)

Neutral threads (piecing blocks)

Contrast thread (top quilting)

Rotary cutter

24" or longer cutting mat

6" x 24" ruler

6" square ruler

Several small postable notes

Chalk or other fabric marker

Transparent fluorescent tape (optional)

3" x 18" ruler (optional)

14" or 9" rotating cutting mat (optional)*

12" x 18" cutting mat (optional)

12½" square ruler (optional)

6½" square ruler (optional)

*Used in this project: Snuggle Up single-sided Microfiber Plush and Hydrangea fabric by Michael Miller and 9" or 14" Boston Revolver rotating cutting mat.

BEFORE BEGINNING Consult the Getting Started section for piecing, sewing and quilting techniques.

 The 90-minute techniques speed up this project, but allow plenty of extra time for specialty fabric preparation, as well as moments to reminisce.

Mohena Belle Harris Butler's 1941 high school graduation photo and the quilt made from her clothing.

PREPARE

1. Collect available clothing. Natural fibers, especially cottons or woven fabrics with a high cotton content, are easiest to work with, but other fabrics can be stabilized so they are easier to use.

2. Sort fabric collection by weight: lightweight (batiste, lightweight cotton, silk or rayon, scarves); medium-weight (heavier cottons, lightweight denim or chambray, medium-weight T-shirt fabrics, lightweight bathrobes or slacks); and heavyweight (denim, suitings, corduroy, sweatshirt fabrics, heavyweight slacks).

3. Select items from either the lightweight and medium-weight piles or from the medium-weight and heavyweight piles to combine in one quilt. Reserve other clothing items for another project.

4. Wash and dry selected clothing. Fragile items may be laundered in lingerie bags.

CUT

1. Cut, as follows:
- 63 squares, 6"x 6", various garment pieces and any additional purchased coordinating fabrics
- 6 strips, 3" x selvage to selvage for border strips, trim selvages

2. Note the following tips for ease in cutting garments:

a. If the garment is large enough, cutting a 12½" square first and then subcutting into 6" squares can save time. Since it can be tricky to accurately cut squares from a garment, the extra ½" allows for a margin of error.

b. Cut side seams, underarm seams and other seams where appropriate on clothing in order to lay the garment flat for cutting squares. Cut on the straight of grain as much as possible.

c. A smaller mat, such as a rotating mat, may be slipped inside clothing to provide a cutting surface when cutting the top layer only.

d. Unruly fabrics, such as T-shirt knits or very lightweight, worn, stretchy or slippery fabrics, can be stabilized with fusible interfacing so they are easier to cut and piece. Cut these fabrics into 6½" squares. Apply a 6⅜" square of fusible interfacing according to manufacturer's instructions. With the interfacing side up, trim to 6" square, cutting through the interfacing so the raw edges of the fabric are "sealed." A rotating mat makes for easier trimming.

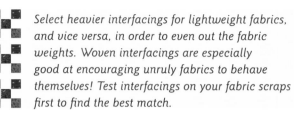

Select heavier interfacings for lightweight fabrics, and vice versa, in order to even out the fabric weights. Woven interfacings are especially good at encouraging unruly fabrics to behave themselves! Test interfacings on your fabric scraps first to find the best match.

e. If the garment is large enough, cut a 13" square, interface with a 12¾" square of fusible interfacing and subcut into four 6" squares.

f. Pockets, seams, tucks, pleats, plackets (including buttons), designer tags, embroidery and other flat garment detailing can be positioned inside the 6" square to add interest to your quilt. Pleats and plackets may be sewn down before cutting. Pockets may be left open.

g. Mix in purchased fabrics with the memory garments. A hydrangea fabric for the 6" blocks was a lucky find! Not only were hydrangeas one of my mother's favorite flowers, the colors in this fabric tied together all the other colors in the quilt.

h. The purchased border fabric was selected for its color relationship to the quilt and the binding. The border required a purchased fabric since there wasn't a piece of clothing large enough from which to cut long strips.

i. The purchased angel fabric was included to commemorate a special event. One of the most extraordinary experiences in my life happened late one night, while my daughter and I were sitting with my mother in  hospice. After hours of motionless quiet, mom suddenly pointed to the ceiling. She looked up and gasped in awe as my daughter and I grabbed each other, transfixed. "Do you see that, all in white?" mom asked us. "Oh, my!" she said, "It's an angel!" Knowingly, my wise daughter high-fived and whispered, "Yay, Gramma!" So, an elegant angel block cut from a Christmas fabric was added to the "ceiling" of the quilt to celebrate that experience.

DESIGN

1. On a large flat surface, place your favorite fabric(s) in prominent places. I started in the center with the square of embroidered denim cut from the back yoke of a shirt, and designed my way out from there. Fill in with other fabrics. The quilt design can be random, or based on specific placement.

2. Position blocks so that any garment detailing, such as seams, pleats or tucks, won't butt up next to each other in adjacent blocks. Rotating or switching blocks can solve this problem. Rebellious fabrics are easier to tame if they are placed next to more obedient fabrics such as a nice, woven cotton.

Pockets, pleats or other interesting details from clothing make use of memorable garments for your own project.

SEW

1. Label and sew the squares into columns.

2. Place the microfiber plush backing on a flat surface, right-side down, smoothing out any wrinkles.

3. Pin the center column 4 and sew all the columns down.

QUILT

Preserve certain squares by stitching around garment detailing on some squares, if you want to maintain the look of the original garment.

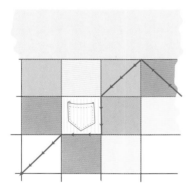

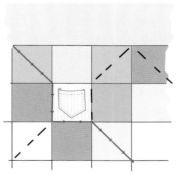

BORDERS

1. Sew together two pairs of 3" x 42" border fabric strips to make two longer strips for the sides.

2. Add the borders.

BIND

1. Trim the backing to 3½" from the raw edge all the way around the pieced top.

2. Use your fingers to roll in the raw edge of the backing ½" on both long sides. Fold backing over the pieced squares. Pin in place, so the backing covers the stay-stitching and at least ⅜" of the raw edge of the pieced blocks. Pin generously.

3. Edgestitch each of the sides. Check edgestitching areas closely to make sure fabrics underneath were caught in the stitches.

4. Repeat steps 2 and 3 for the top and bottom of the quilt.

Detail of Snuggle Up microfiber plush binding on corner.

89

African Goddess

Master all of the 90-minute techniques while you make this easy wall hanging. Slip a small cafe curtain rod through the self-rod pocket to hang.

Finished size: 18" square
(2 x 2 squares plus border)

YOU WILL NEED

½ yd. (or more, if needed to obtain selected motifs) of African goddess motif fabric (blocks)

¾ yd. mottled brick red flannel (backing/binding)

¼ yd. animal skin print fabric (border)

⅝ yd. fleece batting*

Thread to match backing (bobbin)

Neutral threads (piecing blocks)

Contrast thread (top quilting)

4 mm and 5 mm hot-fix crystals in assorted colors*

Hot-fix applicator wand*

Rotary cutter

24" or longer cutting mat

8½" x 24" ruler

6" x 24" ruler

6" square ruler

Several small postable notes

Transparent fluorescent tape (optional)

3" x 18" ruler (optional)

14" or 9" rotating cutting mat (optional)*

*Used in this project: Warm Fleece by the Warm Company (batting); EZ Glitz HotFix Swarovski Crystals by OESD; EZ Glitzer Applicator Wand by OESD; and 14" or 9" Brooklyn Revolver rotating cutting mat by Come Quilt with Me.

BEFORE BEGINNING Consult the Getting Started section for piecing, sewing and quilting techniques.

CUT

1. 4 squares, 6" x 6", fussy-cut African goddess fabric.

2. Cut, as follows:
- 1 square, 25" x 25", mottled brick red flannel
- 1 square, 22" x 22", firm fleece
- 2 strips, 3" x 42", border fabric strips

LAYOUT

Arrange the four African goddess squares following the quilt Layout on page 92 for the same look as shown.

ASSEMBLE

Sew, quilt and add the borders following the instructions on page 30.

BIND

Trim the backing to 3½" and the batting to 1¼". Follow the Self-Binding instructions on page 23.

FINISH

Embellish as desired with hot-fix crystals.

QUILT LAYOUT

APPLYING HOT-FIX CRYSTALS

1. Select and attach 4 mm attachment tip to hot-fix applicator wand. Plug in to preheat.

2. Follow the manufacturer's instructions to adhere 4 mm crystals. Most instructions for hot-fix applicator wands direct the consumer to place the tip onto the crystal, pick it up as shown, watch for the heat-sensitive adhesive on the back to bubble, and place the crystal onto the item to be embellished.

3. Cool, change the tip and repeat to adhere or other size crystals.

The technique described is meant to ensure that delicate fabrics don't get burned with the hot applicator wand. For cotton surfaces that are not likely to be damaged by the heat, this is a quicker and easier way:

1. Place crystal on item to be decorated in position desired.

2. Hold the preheated wand vertically and place it onto the crystal, as shown.

3. Hold down for a count of five to 10 seconds. (The exact amount of time may differ. Practice on scraps to determine the optimum amount of time for the wand and crystals you are using before embellishing your wall hanging.)

4. Remove wand. If the crystal sticks to the wand, slide a pin through the open groove to hold the crystal down while removing the wand.

Use the hot-fix applicator wand to adhere crystals as a quick and attractive way to embellish quilts and wall hangings.

Dogs and Bones

This wall hanging is designed for beginners. The example shown was made by 8-year-old Amanda Schlueter!

Finished size: 18″ square
(2 x 2 squares plus border)

YOU WILL NEED

⅜ yd. (or more, if needed to obtain selected motifs) dog motif fabric

¼ yd. contrast light blue bone fabric

¾ yd. light blue flannel (backing/binding)

¼ yd. beige fabric (border)

22" square fleece batting*

Thread to match backing (bobbin)

Neutral threads (piecing blocks)

Contrast thread (top quilting)

Rotary cutter

24" or longer cutting mat

6" x 24" ruler

6" square ruler

Several small postable notes

Colored chalk or fabric marker

Transparent fluorescent tape (optional)

3" x 18" ruler (optional)

*Used in this project: Warm Fleece by The Warm Company (batting).

BEFORE BEGINNING Consult the Getting Started section for piecing, sewing and quilting techniques.

CUT

1. Child: Select the two dog motifs desired and place 6" ruler over. Trace a 6" square with chalk marker and cut out with child appropriate scissors. Repeat to cut two 6" squares from the contrast bone fabric.

2. Adult: Rotary cut border strips, batting and backing, as follows:
- 1 square, 25" x 25", flannel
- 1 square, 22" x 22", batting
- 2 strips, 3" x 42", border fabric strips

SEW

1. Attach walking foot or engage even feed mechanism to sewing machine.

2. Adult: Use a colored chalk/fabric marker to mark a ⅜" or ½" seam allowance on the wrong side of the two top squares before pinning, so the young sewer can follow this stitching line. It is not necessary for new sewers to use an exact ¼" seam allowance for this project. Larger seam allowances are easier to manage and will simply result in a slightly smaller wall hanging. Once seam allowance has been selected, use that same seam allowance on all remaining seams in the project.

3. Sew, quilt and add the borders following the instructions on page 32.

If center seams don't line up, just embellish with a decorative button! Remember: So-called "mistakes" are simply learning experiences; perfect stitching skills are much less important than having a good time.

BIND

Adult: Rotary cut backing to 3½" and batting to 1¼". Follow the Self-Binding instructions on page 23. Allow the child to participate in pinning and stitching as much as they are able.

The less experience in sewing, the larger the seam allowance. More experienced young sewers may want to use the side of the walking foot as their guide, and may not need chalk lines.

Meryl Ann helps Amanda Schlueter fussy-cut squares for her Dogs and Bones wall hanging. Photo by Photographs by Susie.

A Wild Toss

The clever pillow back has a no-sew finished edge; just pop in a pillow form. Make a quick pillow cover to match your quilt!

Finished size: 14" square
(2 x 2 squares plus borders)

For these and any other pillow covers: If you want a fuller look, remove pillow-form, wrap some batting around it, and reinsert.

YOU WILL NEED

(4) ⅛ yd. animal-skin print flannel (blocks) or leftover blocks from Call of the Wild

¼ yd. dark brown waleless corduroy or cotton velveteen (border)

½ yd. dark brown cotton fabric (backing)

16" square batting*

½ yd. muslin or flannel (will not show)

Thread to match backing (bobbin)

Neutral threads (piecing blocks)

Contrast thread (top quilting)

16" soft or 14" firm pillow form

Rotary cutter

24" or longer cutting mat

8½" x 24" ruler

Several small postable notes

Transparent fluorescent tape (optional)

3" x 18" ruler (optional)

6" square ruler (optional)

*Used in this project: 60/40 Blend by Fairfield (batting)

BEFORE BEGINNING Consult the Getting Started section for piecing, sewing and quilting techniques.

CUT

1. Cut, as follows:
- 1 square, 6" x 6", from each animal-skin flannel print flannel
- 2 strips, 2¾" x 42", dark brown waleless corduroy
- 2 rectangles, 14½" x 19", dark brown cotton fabric
- 1 square, 16" x 16", muslin or flannel
- 1 square, 16" x 16", batting

SEW

Sew, quilt and add the borders, following the instructions on page 32.

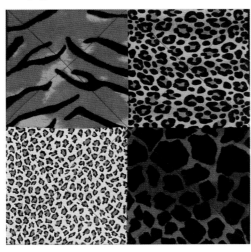

FINISH

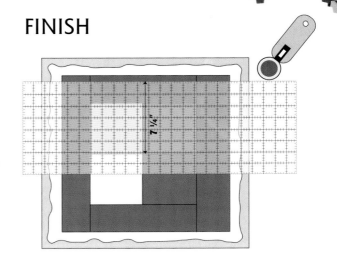

1. Trim the quilted pillow top to 14½" square by using an 8½" x 24" ruler to measure 7¼" from center seams.

2. Fold the dark brown cotton backing pieces, wrong sides together, and press. The folded pieces should measure 9½" x 14½"

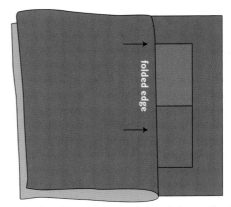

3. Place the backing pieces on top of the quilted pillow top, right sides together, and pin in place.

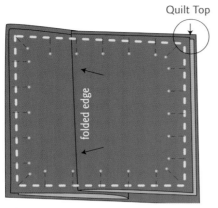

Quilt Top

folded edge

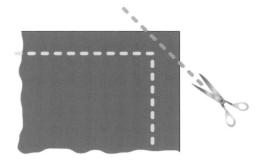

4. Stitch all around pillow with ¼" seam, using the needle down function and lifting the presser foot to pivot at corners.

5. Remove pins and clip corners.

6. Turn right-side out, poke corners out with closed scissors, if needed, and insert pillow form.

On Track

This is a simple variation of A Wild Toss pillow. Vary the fabric selection, fussy-cut the fabric to capture the train motifs and then follow the same assembly instructions as detailed for A Wild Toss.

YOU WILL NEED

⅝ yd. green fabric (border and backing)

⅓ yd. train fabric (or enough yardage to get the two motifs you want)

¼ yd. train track fabric

Additional supplies as used in A Wild Toss

BEFORE BEGINNING Consult the Getting Started section for piecing, sewing and quilting techniques.

INSTRUCTIONS

1. Fussy-cut, as follows:
- 2 squares, 6" x 6", train fabric
- 2 squares, 6" x 6", train track fabric

2. Cut, as follows:
- 2 strips, 2¾" x width of fabric, trim selvages, green fabric
- 2 rectangles, 14½" x 19", green fabric

3. Follow Sew and Finish instructions from A Wild Toss.

Paris in Springtime

This lovely pillow variation is perfect for the boudoir.

YOU WILL NEED

Pink Eiffel Tower fabric (enough to cut two motifs)*

Black Eiffel Tower fabric (enough to cut two motifs)*

⅝ yd. white-and-black cotton print (border and backing)

Additional supplies as used in A Wild Toss

*Used in this project: Eiffel Tower fabric by Michael Miller.

BEFORE BEGINNING Consult the Getting Started section for piecing, sewing and quilting techniques.

CUT

1. Use 6″ square ruler to fussy-cut as follows:

2 squares, 6″ x 6″, pink Eiffel Tower fabric and 2 squares black Eiffel Tower fabric.

a. Place two pieces of household transparent tape on the ruler, over strategic areas of the motif.

b. Trace the outline with a fine point marker and use this as a guide to line the ruler up and quickly and accurately to cut additional squares.

c. Remove tape from the ruler after cutting all the squares.

2. Cut, as follows:

- 2 strips, 2¾″ x 42″/44″ (width of the fabric), white-and-black cotton print

- 2 rectangles, 14½″ x 19″, white-and-black cotton print

3. Follow the Sew and Finish instructions from A Wild Toss with the exception that this pillow may be quilted with outline quilting, by following the lines of the Eiffel Tower motif.

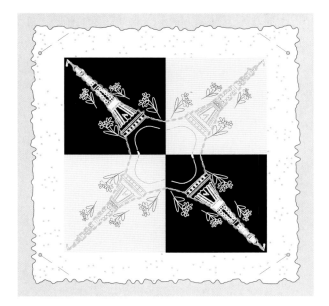

Tic-Tac-Toe

This easy nine-patch is a colorful piece of wall art to display in a game room or kids' room. Just take it off the wall to play! Glow-in-the-dark fabric adds "kid appeal," and a coordinating drawstring bag holds the X's and O's when the game is not in use.

Finished size: 23½" square
(3 x 3 squares plus border)

YOU WILL NEED

¼ yd. off-white glow-in-the-dark fabric or plain off-white fabric (blocks)*

¼ yd. pastel blue-and-green tie-dye fabric (blocks)*

¼ yd. pastel pink-and-orange tie-dye fabric (blocks)*

6" square yellow fabric (center block)

¼ yd. medium value rainbow-colored batik fabric (borders)

⅞ yd. darker value rainbow-colored flannel (backing)*

Fat quarter coordinating fabric (drawstring bag)

29" square fleece batting*

Thread to match backing (bobbin)

Neutral threads (piecing blocks)

Contrast thread (top quilting)*

1 yd. ½"- to 1½"-wide yellow grosgrain or other ribbon

5 plastic bangle bracelets (O's)

5 pairs colored wooden craft sticks (X's)

Craft glue*

Bodkin or large safety pin

Rotary cutter

24" or longer cutting mat

6" x 24" ruler

Several small postable notes

Chalk or other fabric marker

Transparent fluorescent tape (optional)

3" x 18" ruler (optional)

*Used in this project: Michael Miller's glow-in-the-dark Fairy Frost Glow (blocks); Caryl Fallert's Aurora Borealis by Benartex, Lightning design, Pink Opal and Blue Opal by Benartex (blocks); Warm Fleece by Warm Company (batting); Fossil Fern flannel by Benartex (backing/binding); Coats & Clark Egyptian Cotton machine quilting thread Size 50 Multicolor #T38 (top quilting thread); and Aleene's Tacky Glue.

BEFORE BEGINNING Consult the Getting Started section for piecing, sewing and quilting techniques.

Hang the game board and bag on the wall for easy storage and a decorative bedroom accent all in one!

CUT

I. Cut, as follows:
- 4 squares, 6" x 6", off-white glow-in-the-dark fabric or plain off-white fabric
- 2 squares, 6" x 6", blue-and-green tie-dye pastel fabric
- 2 squares, 6" x 6", pink-and-orange tie-dye pastel fabric
- 2 strips, 3" x 42" strips from medium rainbow batik fabric in medium rainbow colors; subcut <u>each</u> into one 3" x 17" strip and one 3" x 21¾" strip, so you end up with two 3" x 17" strips and two 3" x 21¾" strips.
- I square, 31" x 31", darker rainbow flannel
- I rectangle, 14" x 20", coordinating fabric

 Cut ribbon ends on the bias to prevent fraying.

LAYOUT

Arrange all of the squares following the Quilt Layout on page 107 for the same look as shown.

 *Enhance the game board by choosing low-contrast, light fabrics for the nine squares. Without the bag and game pieces, this nine-patch wall hanging can feature contrasting fabrics. Five squares of fussy-cut motif fabric with four squares of a tone-on-tone print make an easy and lively wall hanging.*

SEW

I. Label and sew the squares into columns.

2. Place the backing on a flat surface, right-side down, smoothing out any wrinkles, and place the batting on top.

3. Pin the center column 3 and sew all columns down.

QUILT

Quilt, using the illustrations on the following page to guide you through each pass. Use thread to match the backing fabric in the bobbin.

BORDERS

Add the two 3" x 17" border strips to the sides and the two 3" x 21¾" border strips to the top and bottom. Follow the Adding Borders instructions on page 21.

BIND

Trim the backing to 2¾" and the batting to 1". Follow the Self-Binding instructions on page 23.

QUILT LAYOUT

QUILTING DIAGRAM

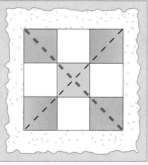

First pass.

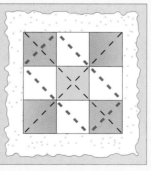

Second pass.

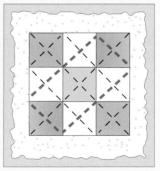

Third pass.

Last pass.

DRAWSTRING BAG

2. Fold fabric in half, right sides together, and stitch across the side and bottom using ¼" seam allowance.

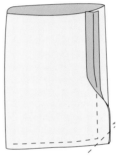

3. Press side seam open halfway down the side. Optional: Use a sleeveboard to press. Clip bottom sewn corner.

4. Fold the top edge down to the chalk line, wrong sides together and pin.

1. Draw a line with chalk marker 1¾" from top long raw edge on the right side of the fat quarter fabric.

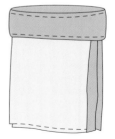

5. Topstitch ¼" from top edge and from bottom raw edge. Turn bag right-side out.

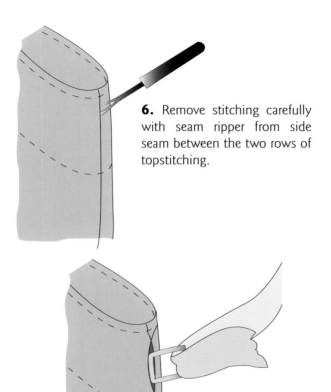

6. Remove stitching carefully with seam ripper from side seam between the two rows of topstitching.

7 With a bodkin or safety pin, pull the ribbon through the casing and tie ribbon ends.

For recyclable gift bags: Cut fabric 18" x 44" for a larger bag or use an 11" x 18" square for a smaller one. These are great for holiday bags. Just stuff them with colored tissue paper and your gift! Use embroidered ribbon, extra-wide sheer ribbon or metallic fabrics for an extra decorative look. Or appliqué or embroider before construction for a designer touch.

MAKE X'S

1. Place a small amount of craft glue on the center of one of the wooden craft sticks.

2. Place another craft stick on top.

3. Repeat steps to make five X's.

4. Allow to dry and store in drawstring bag with the O's.

My Dolly's Quilt

*A perfect size for 12" dolls
(or little stuffed lambs like
the one shown, courtesy
of Carol's Zoo), this
conversation quilt is also a
matching game.*

Finished size: 14" x 19"
5" x 7" mini squares

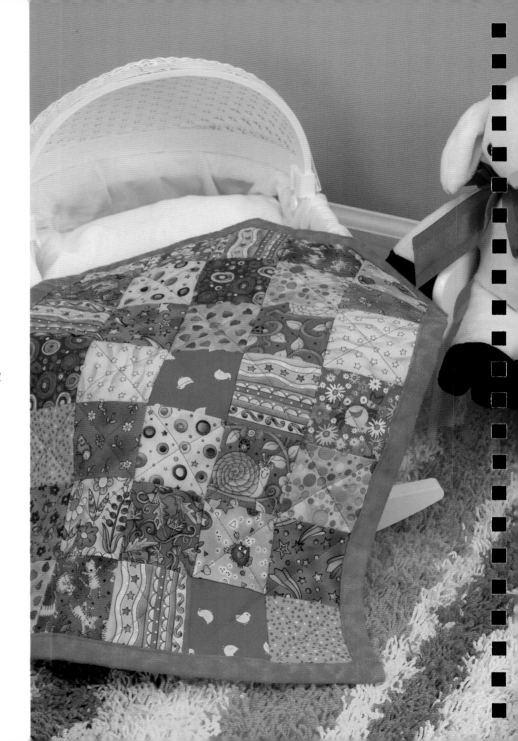

YOU WILL NEED

Scraps or leftover 6" squares of 18 different colorful conversation print fabrics (blocks)

⅝ yd. bright pink flannel (backing)

18" x 23" batting*

Thread to match backing (bobbin)

Neutral threads (piecing blocks)

Contrast thread (top quilting)

Rotary cutter

24" or longer cutting mat

3", 3½" or 6" square ruler

Several small postable notes

Transparent fluorescent tape (optional)

3" x 18" ruler (optional)

14" or 9" rotating cutting mat (optional)*

*Used in this project: Thermore by Hobbs and 14" or 9" Brooklyn Revolver by Come Quilt with Me.

BEFORE BEGINNING Consult the Getting Started section for piecing, sewing and quilting techniques.

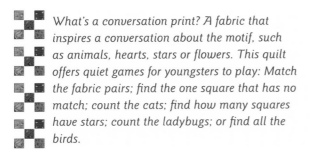 *What's a conversation print? A fabric that inspires a conversation about the motif, such as animals, hearts, stars or flowers. This quilt offers quiet games for youngsters to play: Match the fabric pairs; find the one square that has no match; count the cats; find how many squares have stars; count the ladybugs; or find all the birds.*

CUT

1. Cut, as follows:
- 2 squares, 3" x 3", red conversation print fabric
- 2 squares, 3" x 3", second red conversation print fabric
- 2 squares, 3" x 3", orange conversation print fabric
- 2 squares, 3" x 3", second orange conversation print fabric
- 2 squares, 3" x 3", yellow conversation print fabric
- 2 squares, 3" x 3", second yellow conversation print fabric
- 2 squares, 3" x 3", green conversation print fabric
- 2 squares, 3" x 3", second green conversation print fabric
- 2 squares, 3" x 3", light blue/turquoise conversation print fabric
- 2 squares, 3" x 3", second light blue/turquoise conversation print fabric
- 2 squares, 3" x 3", medium blue conversation print fabric
- 2 squares, 3" x 3", dark blue conversation print fabric
- 2 squares, 3" x 3", fuchsia conversation print fabric
- 2 squares, 3" x 3", multicolor stripe conversation print fabric
- 2 squares, 3" x 3", second multicolor stripe conversation print fabric
- 2 squares, 3" x 3", purple conversation print fabric
- 2 squares, 3" x 3", second purple conversation print fabric
- 1 square, 3" x 3", third purple conversation print fabric
- 1 rectangle, 20" x 26", bright pink flannel

SPEEDY 6" SQUARES METHOD

If you prefer to use up leftover 6" squares, this method speeds up the process and works well for a quilt this size. Nine 6" squares are needed to make a 35-square doll quilt. This method yields four squares from each fabric. Here's how:

1. Place two different 6" squares right sides together.

2. Stitch together opposite sides with ¼" seam allowance.

4. Repeat steps 1 through 3 with additional fabrics until you have enough to make the size quilt you want.

5. Stitch together into columns, interspersing single 3" squares, as desired, and continue to sew the columns down.

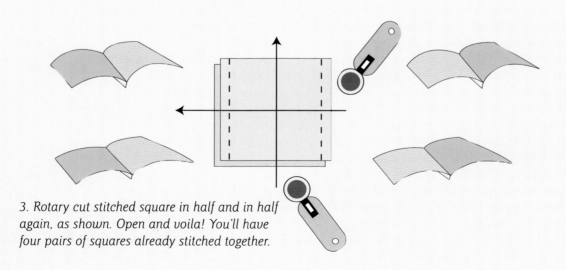

3. Rotary cut stitched square in half and in half again, as shown. Open and voila! You'll have four pairs of squares already stitched together.

LAYOUT

Arrange all the squares following the Quilt Layout for the same look.

SEW

1. Label and sew the squares into columns.

2. Place the backing on a flat surface, right-side down, smoothing out any wrinkles, and roughly center the batting on top.

3. Pin the center column 3 and sew all columns down.

QUILT

Quilt, using thread to match the backing fabric in the bobbin.

BIND

Trim the backing to 1¾" and the batting to ½". Follow the Self-Binding section on page 23.

QUILT LAYOUT

All Dolled Up

Just right for 18" Colonial dolls, this Early American style quilt is made using a quick bargello technique.

Finished size: 19" x 24"
7" x 9" mini squares

YOU WILL NEED

⅛ yd. medium tan #1 Early American-look mini print (blocks)*

⅛ yd. dark red Early American-look mini print (blocks)*

⅛ yd. medium red Early American-look mini print (blocks)*

⅛ yd. rose Early American-look mini print (blocks)*

⅛ yd. pale tan with tiny red stars Early American-look mini print (blocks)*

⅛ yd. medium tan #2 Early American-look mini print (blocks)*

⅛ yd. navy Early American-look mini print (blocks)*

⅛ yd. medium blue Early American-look mini print (blocks)*

⅛ yd. pale tan with tiny blue stars Early American-look mini print (blocks)*

¾ yd. tan flannel (backing)*

25" x 30" thin batting*

Thread to match backing (bobbin)

Neutral threads (piecing blocks)

Contrast quilting thread (top quilting)*

Rotary cutter

24" or longer cutting mat

3" x 18" ruler

16" x 24" ruler

Several small postable notes

Transparent fluorescent tape (optional)

*Used in this project: Early American-look fabrics (blocks) and tan flannel (backing) by P & B Textiles; Thermore by Hobbs (batting); and Isacord Blue #3643 (quilting thread).

BEFORE BEGINNING Consult the Getting started section for piecing, sewing and quilting techniques.

CUT

1. Cut one 3" strip from each of the block fabrics, as follows:

- Medium tan mini print (strip 1)
- Dark red mini print (strip 2)
- Medium red Early American-look mini print (strip 3)
- Rose mini print (strip 4)
- Pale tan with tiny red stars mini print (strip 5)
- Medium tan mini print (strip 6)
- Navy mini print (strip 7)
- Medium blue mini print (strip 8)
- Pale tan with tiny blue stars mini print (strip 9)

2. Trim flannel backing to 26" x 31".

SEW

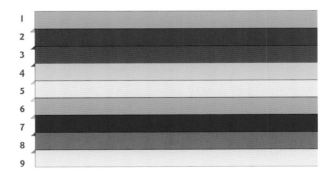

1. Stitch the block fabric strips 1 through 9 together in the order given in step 1 of the Cut section.

2. Press seam allowances down.

3. Fold right sides together. Stitch strip 1 and strip 9 together along raw edges, right sides together, making a tube.

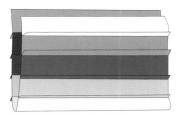

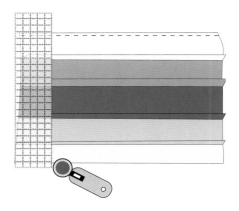

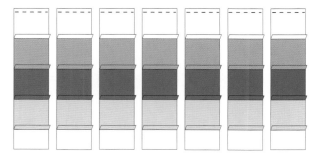

4. Cut seven 3"-wide fabric rings.

5. Create columns by removing stitching with a seam ripper, as follows:
- Ring 1: between strip 1 and strip 9
- Ring 2: between strip 9 and strip 8
- Ring 3: between strip 8 and strip 7
- Ring 4: between fabric 7 and fabric 6
- Ring 5: between fabric 6 and fabric 5
- Ring 6: between fabric 5 and fabric 4
- Ring 7: between fabric 4 and fabric 3
- Ring 8: between fabric 3 and fabric 2
- Ring 9: between fabric 2 and fabric 1

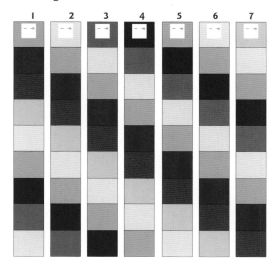

6. Lay out columns in order.

7. Label the columns and press the seam allowances with even-numbered columns up and odd-numbered columns down.

8. Place the backing on a flat surface, right-side down, smoothing out any wrinkles, and place the batting on top.

9. Pin the center column 4 and sew all columns down.

QUILT

Quilt, using thread to match the backing fabric in the bobbin.

BIND

Trim the backing to 1¾" and the batting to ½". Follow the Self-Binding instructions on page 23.

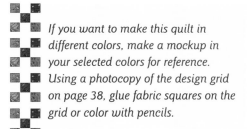

If you want to make this quilt in different colors, make a mockup in your selected colors for reference. Using a photocopy of the design grid on page 38, glue fabric squares on the grid or color with pencils.

QUILT LAYOUT

Check Mate

This easy checkerboard makes a great wall hanging for a game room or kids' room. Just take it off the wall to play! A clever fabric envelope buttons to the back and holds the checkers, so the board and game pieces are always together.

Finished size: 21" square
(8 x 8 mini squares)

YOU WILL NEED

⅜ yd. predominantly black with small all-over random print (blocks)

⅜ yd. predominantly red with small all-over random print (blocks)

¾ yd. yellow print flannel (backing/binding)

(2) 26" squares stiff batting*

9" x 12" piece Kelly green all wool or wool blend felt (checkers)*

9" x 12" piece royal blue all wool or wool blend felt (checkers)*

9" x 12" yellow all wool or wool blend felt (checkers case)*

½" to ¾" smiley face shank button*

Thread to match backing (bobbin)*

Red thread (piecing blocks)

Contrast thread (top quilting)

Rotary cutter

24" or longer cutting mat

6" x 24" ruler

Several small postable notes

Transparent fluorescent tape (optional)

3" x 18" ruler (optional)

*Used in this project: Two layers Soft and Black fleece by the Warm Company; wool blend felt by National Nonwovens (checkers and case); yellow thread by Isacord (top and bobbin thread); button by Blumenthal-Lansing and Olfa Circle Cutter.

BEFORE BEGINNING Consult the Getting Started section for piecing, sewing and quilting techniques.

For a nontraditional look, choose wild colors for the checkerboard, such as hot pink and neon green with purple and yellow checkers.

Hang the checkerboard on the wall when not in use for easy storage and a decorative wall accent all in one!

CUT

I. Cut, as follows:
- 4 strips, 3" wide, black print fabric
- 4 strips, 3" wide, red print fabric

2. Trim flannel to 27" square.

SEW

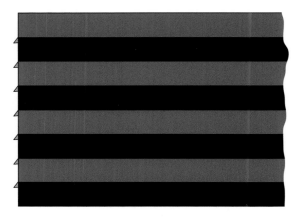

1. Stitch the eight strips together along the long edge, right sides together, with ¼" seam allowance, alternating black with red to create a stripped unit as shown.

2. Press seams allowances down.

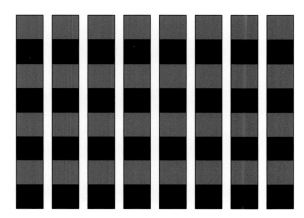

3. Crosscut eight 3"-wide strips from the stripped unit.

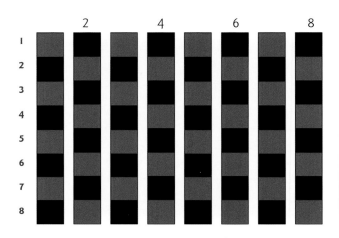

4. Reverse columns 2, 4, 6 and 8, so the bottom square of each column is now at the top. This creates the checkerboard pattern.

5. Pin numbered postable notes to the tops of each column.

6. Place the backing on a flat surface, right-side down, smoothing out any wrinkles, and place batting on top.

7. Line up the right side of column 4 with the center of the wall hanging and pin. Sew all the columns down.

QUILT

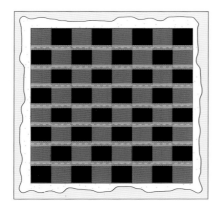

1. Quilt by stitching in the ditch with red thread and bobbin thread to match the backing on seven horizontal seams only. Backstitch at the beginning and ends of quilting lines. If any red stitches go astray on the black fabric, don't remove them, just color them in with a black permanent marker.

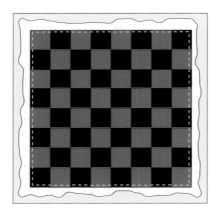

2. Staystitch ¼" from raw edge of pieced squares.

BIND

1. Trim the backing to 1¾" and the batting to ½". Follow the Self-Binding section on page 23.

2. Sew the button onto back of the checkerboard 1½" below the edgestitching, passing needle and thread through batting, but not through to front of quilt.

CHECKERBOARD LAYOUT

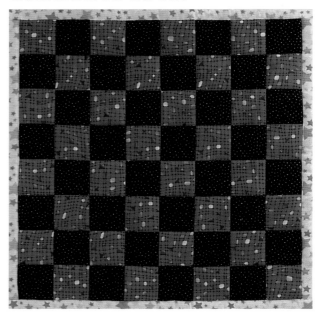

MAKE CHECKERS

1. Cut (14) 2"-diameter circles from green and blue wool felt, using one of the following methods:

a. Use an Olfa circle cutter: Follow manufacturer's instructions on package to set cutter; tape felt to cutting board at corners to prevent slippage; and cut circles, as shown.

b. Make a 2"-diameter template on heavy paper or template plastic, trace onto the felt and cut the circles individually by hand.

 Just 12 checkers of each color are needed to play the game, but cutting additional checkers of each color allows for spares in case of lost pieces.

MAKE CHECKER POUCH

1. Cut 6" x 12" piece from yellow felt.

2. Fold ends in 1½" and press with iron at temperature appropriate for fiber content of wool blend.

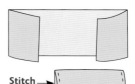

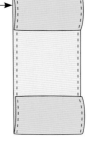

3. Stitch ¼" from edge on top and bottom, backstitching at beginning and end.

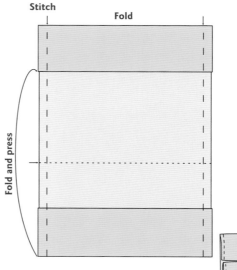

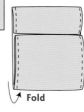

4. Fold one end in toward the center and press.

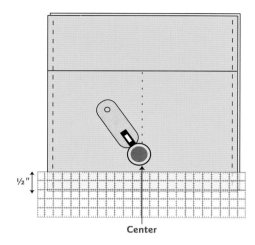

½"

Center

Fill with checkers.

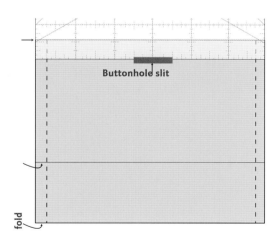

Buttonhole slit

fold

5. Cut buttonhole slit with rotary cutter ½" from fold.

6. Fill the pouch with checkers and button it to the back of the checkerboard for storage.

It's In the Bag

This quick shoulder bag or mini-tote introduces kids to the machine and gives them sewing confidence! The stability of flannel makes it forgiving to sew with, and the project can be completed in a few minutes or use specialty fabrics for a quick and easy chatelaine.

Finished size: 5" to 5½" square

YOU WILL NEED

(2) 6" or 6½" squares flannel (matching or coordinating)

1 yd. (shoulder bag) or 12" (mini-tote) ½" to ⅝"-wide grosgrain ribbon

Thread

Age-appropriate iron*

Scissors or rotary cutter

Chalk or other fabric marker

Sleeveboard (optional)

*Used in the project: Clover mini-iron.

BEFORE BEGINNING Consult the Getting Started section for piecing, sewing and quilting techniques.

Shorten the ribbon handle and change the fabric to create a mini-tote variation for a boy.

SEW

1. Use chalk or fabric marker to make a line on the right side of each 6″ (6½″) fabric square, ½″ from one raw edge, on both squares.

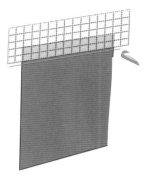

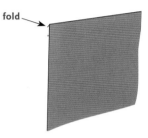

fold

2. Fold down along the top edge of both squares, wrong sides together, along chalk line and press.

3. Topstitch folded edge of both squares. Exact distance from fold is determined by using the edge of sewing foot as a guide.

4. Place squares right sides together, lining up stitched edges.

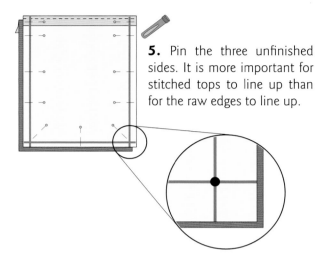

5. Pin the three unfinished sides. It is more important for stitched tops to line up than for the raw edges to line up.

6. Mark seamline with chalk and ruler, marking large dots at two intersections. Select ½″, ⅜″ or ¼″ seam allowance based on sewer's experience level.

7. Backstitch at beginning of the seam, stitch along three raw edges and backstitch at the end. Use needle-down function, if available, and pivot at large dots.

FINISH

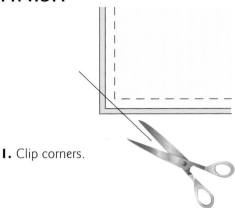

1. Clip corners.

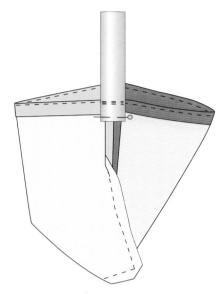

3. Pin ribbon to inside of seam on one side.

4. Topstitch ribbon handle to bag by following previous stitching on bag, backstitching several times for strength.

5. Pin ribbon to other side, making sure ribbon isn't twisted. Try on, shortening ribbon, if desired.

6. Stitch as in step 4.

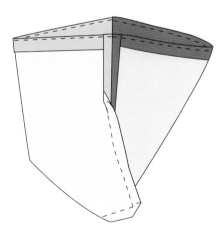

2. Press open top portion of seam allowance, about 2″ down from top of bag. Use sleeveboard for ease in pressing. This pressing maneuver is a bit tricky, and may be a more appropriate job for the adult in charge, unless the young sewer is an experienced presser.

Machine-Embroidered Silk Heirloom

This stunning heirloom is a perfect project for experienced machine embroiderers who don't want to spend a lot of time on quilting, since the 90-Minute Quilts techniques make it quick to construct. The luxurious fabrics are perfect for creating keepsake baby gifts, such as for a christening. Guest artist and Bernina fashion designer Susan Deal did the beautiful embroidery for this project.

Finished size: 32" x 43"
(5 x 7 squares plus borders)

YOU WILL NEED

Quilting Supplies

2 yd. sage duppioni silk (embroidered squares)

2 yd. peach duppioni silk (embroidered squares)

⅜ yd. 42"-wide natural color silk noil (borders)

⅝ yd. natural tan duppioni silk (bias binding)

1¼ yd. lightweight fusible interfacing (backing)

1⅜ yd. 42"-wide cotton flannel, silk broadcloth or China silk (backing)

36" x 48" batting*

Thread to match backing (bobbin)

Neutral threads (piecing blocks)

Clear polyester thread (top quilting)*

Rotary cutter

24" or longer cutting mat

6" x 24" ruler

6" square ruler

Several small postable notes

Transparent fluorescent (optional)

3" x 18" ruler (optional)

14" or 9" rotating cutting mat (optional)*

Machine Embroidery Supplies

Embroidery machine and hoops

Machine embroidery thread*

Embroidery designs of choice*

62 white 11" x 14" pieces cut-away stabilizer*

4 yd. fusible tricot interfacing*

(31) 9" x 12" pieces very lightweight batting (embroidery)*

Temporary adhesive spray*

Bobbin thread (embroidery)

*Used in this project: Matilda's Own wool batting; MonoPoly clear polyester thread by Superior Threads; 14" or 9" Boston Revolver rotating cutting mat; Isacord machine embroidery thread in #0101 off-white, #5552 sage and #1060 peach; OESD embroidery designs from Angel NY221, Butterfly NY210 and symmetrical lace design NY218. Dragonfly NX690; OESD PolyMesh Cut-Away Stabilizer; Handlers Fusible Tricot Interfacing; Hobbs Thermore Batting; and OESD 505 Spray and Fix.

BEFORE BEGINNING Consult the Getting Started section for piecing, sewing and quilting techniques.

CUT

1. Back all of the silks before cutting to give strength and stability to the duppioni and to help avoid fraying. Even nonembroidered squares can benefit from this process to create more regularity in weight. They were layered as follows: silk, interfacing, batting and two layers of PolyMesh on top. Simpler designs with fewer stitches might require only one layer of stabilizer. The butterfly, angel and symmetrical lace design were reduced/enlarged/etc. in the software on the computer before sending to the machine, since the computer has a faster processor.

2. Cut, as follows:

- 17 sage duppioni silk squares cut to fit your hoop; these were cut 10" x 12"
- 4 squares, 6" x 6", sage duppioni, corner squares (these will not be embroidered)
- 14 peach duppioni silk squares cut to fit your hoop; these were cut 10" x 12"
- 4 strips, 2¾" x 42", silk noil border (back the fabric with fusible interfacing before cutting)
- 1 rectangle, 38" x 49", cotton flannel, silk broadcloth or China silk backing

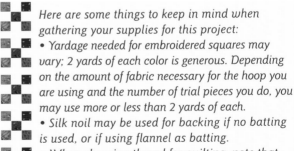

Here are some things to keep in mind when gathering your supplies for this project:

• Yardage needed for embroidered squares may vary; 2 yards of each color is generous. Depending on the amount of fabric necessary for the hoop you are using and the number of trial pieces you do, you may use more or less than 2 yards of each.

• Silk noil may be used for backing if no batting is used, or if using flannel as batting.

• When choosing thread for quilting, note that nylon filament is difficult to work with and is not recommended as a substitute for clear polyester thread.

EMBROIDER

1. Machine-embroider silk squares as desired or stitch the following to achieve the same look shown:

- one center block angel on sage silk with off-white thread
- six butterflies on sage silk with peach thread
- 10 dragonflies on sage silk with peach thread
- 14 symmetrical lace designs on peach silk with sage thread

Note: Before embroidering, the orientation of the dominant weave of the duppioni was alternated to enhance the luster of the silk. The direction of the weave of all of the peach blocks and the four unembroidered sage blocks were oriented vertically. The weave on the 17 remaining blocks with the angel, butterfly and dragonfly embroidered designs was oriented horizontally.

2. Leave four sage blocks unembroidered.

3. Unhoop, press and trim away batting and mesh stabilizer from each block after the design stitching is complete.

4. Trim each embroidered block to 6" square, using the center markings on the ruler and/or the center marking on the design printout as a guide to center the design. A rotating mat is useful for trimming.

LAY OUT

Arrange all the squares on a flat design surface, following the Quilt Layout on page 132 for the look shown.

SEW

1. Label and sew the squares into columns.

2. Place the backing on a flat surface, right-side down, smoothing out any wrinkles, and place batting on top.

3. Pin the center column 3 and sew all columns down.

Note: If using China silk or other slippery backing, pin very generously and hold taut while sewing to prevent slippage and unwanted pleats.

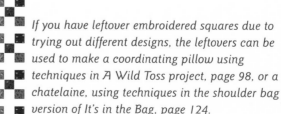

If you have leftover embroidered squares due to trying out different designs, the leftovers can be used to make a coordinating pillow using techniques in A Wild Toss project, page 98, or a chatelaine, using techniques in the shoulder bag version of It's in the Bag, page 124.

QUILT

Quilt by stitching in the ditch with MonoPoly thread and bobbin thread to match the backing on six horizontal seams only. Backstitch at the beginning and ends of quilting lines. These quilting stitches enhance the loft but don't interfere with the embroidery.

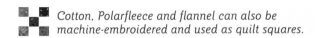 *Cotton, Polarfleece and flannel can also be machine-embroidered and used as quilt squares.*

FINISH

1. Add the four 2¾"-wide border strips. Follow the instructions for Adding Borders on page 21.

2. Pin raw edges down.

3. Staystitch ¼" in from the raw edge of the border strips around the entire perimeter.

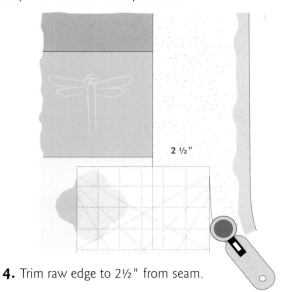

2 ½"

4. Trim raw edge to 2½" from seam.

5. Cover raw edges with bias binding, using preferred method or the Making Bias Binding instructions as shown on page 26.

Detail of finished edge of the quilt.

Velvet Meditations

Cuddle up by a fire to read or meditate under this luxurious velvet throw. With a cozy backing of black silk noil it feels as luscious as it looks.

Finished size: 49" x 70"
(9 x 13 squares)

YOU WILL NEED

⅝ yd. <u>total</u> (or enough fabric for (18) 6" squares) purple/violet/plum/fuchsia color family assorted pile fabrics (blocks)

⅝ yd. <u>total</u> (or enough fabric for (18) 6" squares) royal blue/navy/denim blue color family assorted pile fabrics (blocks)

⅝ yd. <u>total</u> (or enough fabric for (18) 6" squares) teal/blue-green/turquoise color family assorted pile fabrics (blocks)

⅝ yd. <u>total</u> (or enough fabric for (18) 6" squares) warm green/Kelly/forest green color family assorted pile fabrics (blocks)

⅜ yd. <u>total</u> (or enough fabric for nine 6" squares) yellows/mustard/golden browns color family assorted pile fabrics (blocks)

⅝ yd. <u>total</u> (or enough fabric for (18) 6" squares) tangerine/sienna/orangey browns color family assorted pile fabrics (blocks)

⅝ yd. <u>total</u> (or enough fabric for (18) 6" squares) reds/rose/fuchsia/maroon color family assorted velvets (blocks)

3⅜ yd. black silk noil (backing) (yardage amount allows for shrinkage)

2 yd. black velveteen (seamless border)

1¼ yd. black poly charmeuse, jacquard or habutai (bias binding)

Thread to match backing (bobbin)

Neutral threads (piecing blocks)

Walking foot or even feed function

Rotary cutter

24" or longer cutting mat

6" x 24" ruler

6" square ruler

Several small postable notes

Transparent fluorescent tape (optional)

3" x 18" ruler (optional)

14" or 9" rotating cutting mat (optional)*

*Used in this project: Silk noil by Thai Silks (backing) and Boston Revolver rotating cutting mat.

CUT

1. Cut as follows:
- 18 squares, 6" x 6", purple/violet/plum/fuchsia assorted pile fabrics
- 18 squares, 6" x 6", royal blue/navy/denim blue assorted pile fabrics
- 18 squares, 6" x 6", teal/blue-green/turquoise assorted pile fabrics
- 18 squares, 6" x 6", warm green/kelly/forest green assorted pile fabrics
- 9 squares, 6" x 6", yellows/mustard/golden browns assorted pile fabrics
- 18 squares, 6" x 6", tangerine/sienna/orangey browns assorted pile fabrics
- 18 squares, 6" x 6", reds/rose/fuchsia/maroon assorted velvets
- 4 strips, 3" x 69" long strips of black velveteen cut the lengthwise grain of fabric

Keep in mind...
- *Assorted pile fabrics include velveteen, velvet, crushed velvet, panne velvets, velour, waleless corduroy and other similar fabrics.*
- *Yardages for block fabrics are generous in that if you had none on hand, you would need the amount listed to obtain (18) 6" squares on 42"-wide fabric, with three extra 6" squares left over. You need enough fabric to cut 117 total 6" squares in various colors.*
- *Less yardage of the velveteen border fabric is needed if seams in the side borders are acceptable.*
- *Less yardage of the fabric for the bias binding is needed if more seams are acceptable.*
- *In order to create the look of this quilt, you will need 35 to 70 different colors.*
- *The width of pile fabrics varies widely, so be sure to check widths when buying yardage.*

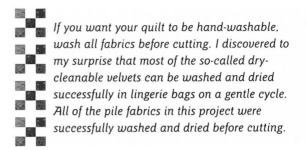

LAY OUT

1. Arrange all the squares in the following order. Refer to the Quilt Layout on page 137 for the same look as shown:

- Rows 1 and 2: reds/rose/fuchsia/maroon color family
- Rows 3 and 4: tangerine/sienna/orange browns color family
- Row 5: yellows, mustard/golden browns
- Rows 6 and 7: warm green/kelly/forest green color family
- Rows 8 and 9: teal/blue-green/turquoise color family
- Rows 10 and 11: royal blue/navy/denim blue color family
- Rows 12 and 13: purple/violet/plum/fuchsia color family

Note: This is a general guide for placement. It's OK if some colors "wander out" of their assigned sections. In fact it's better if a few squares do so to keep the color flow from looking too regimented.

COLLECTING PILE FABRICS

Amassing a collection of velvets can take some time, but it is fun! A good time to purchase velvets, velveteens and other pile fabrics is after the winter holidays when they are often on sale. Printed, embossed and embroidered pile fabrics work well also. Velvet scraps may be available from previous sewing projects. Sources of velvet may be discovered in surprising places: an old velveteen bathrobe and a pair of velvet slacks, both no longer usable due to worn areas, can yield a wealth of 6" squares! Garments from thrift shops can be especially valuable, as they often feature hard-to-find colors that were popular in former seasons. Some pile upholstery fabrics are lightweight enough for this quilt. Cotton velveteen is the most stable of these pile fabrics, a higher proportion of velveteen squares makes this throw easier to sew.

If you want your quilt to be hand-washable, wash all fabrics before cutting. I discovered to my surprise that most of the so-called dry-cleanable velvets can be washed and dried successfully in lingerie bags on a gentle cycle. All of the pile fabrics in this project were successfully washed and dried before cutting.

SEW

1. Move the needle to the far left position, as velvets and other pile fabrics require a seam allowance larger than ¼" to allow for fraying. This also has the advantage of putting the seam allowance closer to the left edge of the foot, so most of the damage to the velvet pile from the foot will be in the seam allowance and not on the right side of the velvet. Use the right edge of the foot as a guide to stitch by, not the lines on your machine bed as you will not be able to see these lines when sewing the strips to the backing. Your seam allowance should be ½" or nearly that. Once you have selected your seam allowance, all remaining seams in the project should be the same seam allowance.

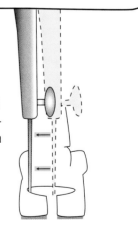

2. Label and sew the squares into columns. Press as you go, following tip information on page 136. Optional but recommended: Zigzag stitch each seam allowance together along the raw edge, if quilt will be washed or otherwise treated vigorously. This has the added advantage of compressing the bulkiness of the seam allowance.

3. Place the backing on a flat surface, right-side down, smoothing out any wrinkles.

4. Pin the center column 5 and sew all columns down. Use the same foot and seam allowance as before.

5. Press each column gently with a thick terry-cloth towel before adding next column to the quilt.

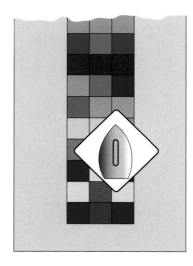

Optional: Fold pieced column (in front) and backing fabric (in back) out of the way so only the seam allowance of the two pieced columns is zigzag stitched. This way, the zigzag stitching will not show on the backing of the quilt.

When sewing with velvet, remember the following tips:

- *Pile needs to be protected during pressing. Use a velvet board or thickly-folded rough terry-cloth towel (folded at least three or four times) as the pressing surface. Place velvet on this surface with the pile side down, and press lightly.*
- *Use thin, sharp pins and pin within seam allowances where possible. Remove pins immediately after stitching. Pin generously if the fabric is slippery.*
- *If the pile of a velvet square gets damaged, slightly crushed from the weight of a presser foot or marred by pins, try spraying it lightly with water and fluffing with a toothbrush to help restore the pile to its original state.*

BORDERS

1. Generously pin raw edges or border strips to quilt top to prevent slippage. Follow the Adding Borders instructions on page 21, sewing strips to long sides first, followed by short sides.

2. Staystitch ¼" in from raw edge of border strips.

3. Trim backing and any excess border fabric 2½" from the seam. If velvet border strip is a little short, it's OK, as long as it falls within ⅝" seam allowance for bias binding.

BIND

Finish with bias binding, as detailed in the Making Bias Binding instructions on page 26.

Silk Sophistication

Toss this elegant shawl over your shoulder to dress up any outfit for the most elegant occasion. Or make one as a luxurious table decoration. What a fabulous gift. Easy faux mitered corners enhance the stunning beauty of the silks and brocades.

Finished size: 25½" x 85½"
(17 x 5 squares)

YOU WILL NEED

¼ yd. <u>each</u> 15 to 28 assorted brocades, silk noil, silk duppioni, cotton prints, metallic printed cotton, cottons woven with lurex or hand-dyed suede-look cotton (blocks)*

2⅝ yd. silk duppioni (backing/binding)

Thread to match backing (bobbin)

Neutral thread (piecing blocks)

MonoPoly thread (top quilting)

Rotary cutter

24" or longer cutting mat

6" x 24" ruler

6" square ruler (optional for fussy-cutting)

Several small postable notes

Tricot fusible interfacing (optional)

Transparent fluorescent tape (optional)

3" x 18" ruler (optional)

*Used in this project: Silk noil, silk duppioni and silk brocades from Thai Silks (blocks) and hand-dyed suede-look cotton from Cherrywood Fabrics.

BEFORE BEGINNING Consult the Getting Started section for piecing, sewing and quilting techniques.

CUT

1. 42 squares, slinky brocades (silk, rayon, poly) 43 squares, stable fabrics (printed cottons, metallic printed cottons, metallic woven cottons, silk noil or silk duppioni.

2. Trim silk duppioni backing to 35" x 94". Reserve trimmings, if large enough, to cut some 6" squares if desired.

- *The shawl will drape nicely without interfacing the squares; however, if you want to include a particularly slinky brocade, it may behave better if backed with a tricot fusible interfacing. If interfacing, apply it following manufacturer's directions before cutting the 6" squares.*

- *Silk duppioni must be dry-cleaned. If you prefer for the shawl to be hand-washable, substitute a washable fabric such as silk noil for the dupioni backing and use only washable fabrics for the squares. Prewash and machine or iron dry all fabrics, including the noil. Noil is too thick for this faux mitered corner technique, so substitute bias binding using polyester jacquard, cotton or other thin, washable fabric.*

- *The yardages given in the materials list assumes a minimum 36" fabric width; however, many specialty fabrics have smaller widths. So be sure when purchasing fabrics that you have enough for the number of squares necessary to complete your design.*

LAY OUT

1. Arrange all the squares following the Shawl Layout on page 143 for the same look as shown. Alternate the orientations of any directional fabrics such as duppioni or stripes. Reposition squares until you like the arrangement. Brocade squares will be easier to sew if <u>at least</u> two sides have a more stable fabric, such as cotton, noil or duppioni next to them.

2. Label columns 1 through 17 and stack.

SEW

1. Move the needle to the far left position, as brocades and duppionis require a seam allowance larger than ¼" to allow for fraying. Use the right edge of the foot as a stitching guide to stitch by, not the lines on your machine bed, as you will not be able to see these lines when sewing the strips to the backing. Your seam allowance should be at least ½" for all seams in this project.

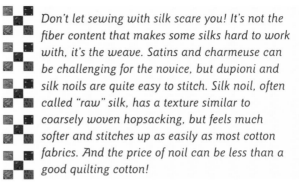

Don't let sewing with silk scare you! It's not the fiber content that makes some silks hard to work with, it's the weave. Satins and charmeuse can be challenging for the novice, but dupioni and silk noils are quite easy to stitch. Silk noil, often called "raw" silk, has a texture similar to coarsely woven hopsacking, but feels much softer and stitches up as easily as most cotton fabrics. And the price of noil can be less than a good quilting cotton!

2. Sew the squares into columns. There will be 17 columns with five squares in each.

3. Press seams using appropriate temperature for fabrics: even-numbered columns up and odd-numbered down.

4. Fold backing in half, wrong sides together, and press. These creases will be measuring guides. Press top edge of backing 5" down from top selvage and open.

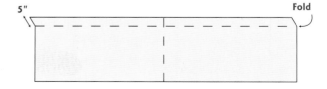

5. Place backing on a flat surface, right-side down, smoothing out any wrinkles.

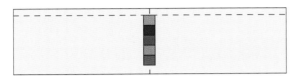

6. Pin the center column 9 to the backing, using the center crease as a placement guide and lining up the top of the column with horizontal crease.

7. Sew all the columns down.

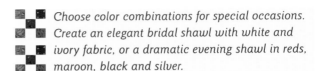

Choose color combinations for special occasions. Create an elegant bridal shawl with white and ivory fabric, or a dramatic evening shawl in reds, maroon, black and silver.

QUILT

1. Use MonoPoly thread for the top thread and thread to match the backing in the bobbin. Stitch a sample on a scrap to check thread tension, adjusting tension, if needed.

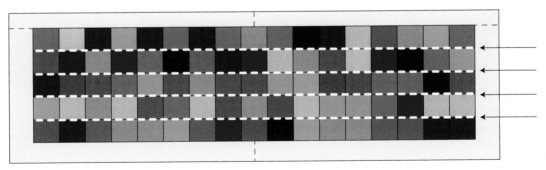

2. Quilt four horizontal quilting lines by stitching in the ditch, backstitching at beginning and end.

BIND

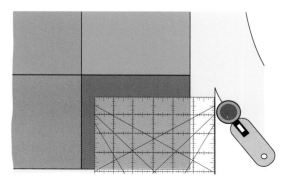

1. Trim the backing binding to 1⅛" from the raw edges of the squares on all four sides.

2. Pin corner squares to stabilize.

3. Fold and press two long sides of backing/binding, wrong sides together, butting up raw edges of backing/binding with raw edges of squares.

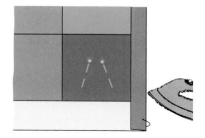

4. Fold again, right sides together, covering raw edges of squares, and press again. Pin, avoiding corners.

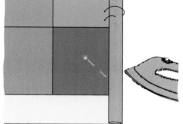

5. Repeat steps 3 and 4 on short sides. Pin and edgestitch for standard corners, or continue with step 6 for faux mitered corners.

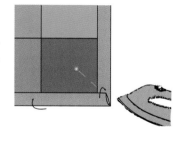

6. Open corner portion of backing/binding by unfolding one fold on both sides of corner.

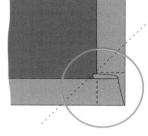

7. Fold corner "A" in, lining up the pressed fold lines of the backing/binding with the raw edges of the squares, as shown. Press along diagonal.

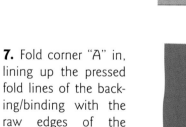

8. Fold one side in, lining up Point B with Point A. Press.

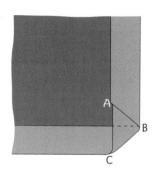

9. Fold Point C up to meet Point A for a perfect faux mitered corner. Press corner and pin. Repeat with remaining three corners.

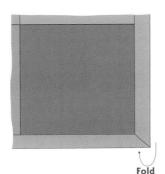

Fold

10. Starting partway down any side (not at a corner), edgestitch close to edge, pivoting at corners and backstitching at beginning and end of stitching. (Or, hand stitch if desired.)

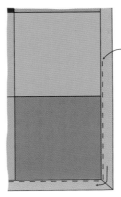

Gallery

Find lots of inspiration for your own 90-Minute Quilts in the gallery. The time saving methods used in these lovely quilts can be adapted to many other projects. So have fun getting creative!

Poinsettias and Holly

Made by: Meryl Ann Butler

Finished size: 42" x 56½" (7 x 9 squares plus border)

Create it: More than 55 different fabrics are featured on this quilt, each one featuring holly or poinsettias. The flannel backing was too short to make a self-binding, so it was trimmed and a bias binding was added. Borders feature decorative machine quilting stitches. Hobbs Heirloom 100% Wool Batting was used and additional quilting was done by stitching in the ditch of the horizontal seams.

144

Pretty in Pink

Made by: Meryl Ann Butler

Finished size: 30" x 41" (5 x 7 squares)

Create it: Jazzy retro prints in sassy colors and a diagonal arrangement make an appealing quilt for a toddler or even a wall hanging for a teen. Flannel backing and fabrics by Timeless Treasures and Touch of Cashmere batting by Mountain Mist.

Flamingo Fun

Made by: Meryl Ann Butler and Trish Schmeidl (design collaboration) with appliqué work and construction by Trish Schmeidl

Finished size: 30" x 41" (5 x 7 squares)

Create it: The flannel backing/binding inspired the flamingo theme. Because this quilt is a wall hanging, no diagonal quilting was needed. Isacord threads, Machine 60/40 Blend Batting by Fairfield and flamingo appliqué pattern by Trish Schmeidl's Threads and Needles.

145

Ride 'em Cowgirl

Made by: Susan Deal

Finished size: 30" x 41" (5 x 7 squares)

Create it: The center square was pieced so that the "buffalo gals" would radiate from the center. The four large cowgirl motifs were cut on the diagonal because if they had been cut on the vertical, they would have been cut off at the knees! The diagonal placement also adds a sense of movement. Cowgirl fabrics by Alexander Henry, Spirit of the West fabric by Maywood Studios, Cowboy Up fabric by Patrick Lose for Timeless Treasures, Madeline flannel by RJR and Warm and Natural batting by the Warm Company.

New Country

Made by: Rali Burleson, Arizona Make It Yourself With Wool director

Finished size: 30" x 41" (5 x 7 squares)

Create it: To accommodate the bulkiness of the wool, the squares in this quilt were cut 6½" so the seam allowances could be enlarged to ½". Seams were pressed open and the columns were offset to avoid intersecting seams. The quilt was tied using perle cotton and vintage Bakelite buttons. Evergreen Inn flannel by RJR and hand overdyed 100-percent wool fabric by Weeks Dye Works.

Ruff and Fluff

Made by: Maria Turner

Finished size: 30" x 41" (5 x 7 squares)

Create it: Twin blues, twin reds and triplet black fabrics add complexity and textural interest in this boldly colored quilt. It was a gift for a newborn baby of a dog-lover dad and cat-lover mom. The child, of course, will love both, thanks to the inspiration she gets from this bright and fun quilt. Machine 60/40 Blend Batting by Fairfield and flannel backing/binding and Ruff 'n Fluff block fabrics by Moda.

All Aboard

Made by: Meryl Ann Butler

Finished size: 39½" x 61" (7 x 11 squares)

Create it: A baker's dozen fabrics featuring trains, tracks and railroad signals choo-choo their way across this lap quilt made for my dad, a model railroad buff. Thai Silks silk noil were used for the blocks and silk noil was used for the backing/binding.

Chandler's Horses

Made by: Chandler Fox

Finished size: 41½" x 52½" (7 x 9 squares)

Create it: Chandler, a talented 10-year-old, designed and made this quilt to coordinate with her new bedroom décor. She fussy-cut 15 horse motif squares and surrounded them with squares in denim and bandana fabrics. This quilt was tied with horse buttons and finished with red Polarfleece backing/binding.

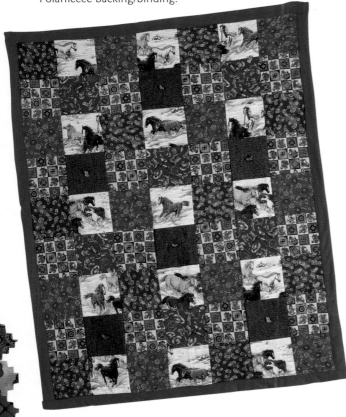

Mola Magic

Made by: Meryl Ann Butler and Trish Schmeidl (design collaboration), with original appliqué work and construction by Trish Schmeidl

Finished size: 30" x 41" (5 x7 squares)

Create it: Beautiful mola embroideries are paired with focus fabric from Robert Kaufman's Guatamalan collection and Freckles from FreeSpirit. Trish, of Trish Schmeidl's Threads and Needles, designed these embroideries so they have no jumps. Because this quilt is a wall hanging, no cross quilting was needed. Isacord thread and Machine 60/40 Blend Batting by Fairfield were used in this quilt.

Pansy Garden

Made by: Meryl Ann Butler

Finished size: 39½" x 61" (7 x 11 squares)

Create it: A true "charm" quilt because it has no repeated fabrics, this snuggle quilt made for my mom features 77 different pansy fabrics collected over several years. Dusty lavender silk noil by Thai Silks was used for backing/binding.

Hanah's Cats

Made by: Meryl Ann Butler

Finished size: 41" x 61" (7 x 9 squares plus border)

Create it: Kitties in sophisticated colors balanced with a black and white woven check make a sassy snuggle quilt for my teen granddaughter. A trip-pieced border at top and bottom adds length. Turquoise silk noil by Thai Silks on the backing and self-binding picks up the color of the kittens' blue collars.

Rainbow's Beginning

Made by: Meryl Ann Butler

Finished size: 30" x 41" (5 x 7 squares)

Create it: A Broad Band Fundamentals gradating stripes by FreeSpirit were cut in seven colorways. Create this quilt with the Faux Rail Fence, techniques on page 62. With this wider band stripe, only two stripes will fit in the 6" square. For added interest, squares were measured and cut with the darker stripe slightly wider than the lighter stripe. Backing/batting is Bali Flanneltik by Princess Mirah Designs.

Half-Square Triangle Quilt

Made by: Meryl Ann Butler

Finished size: 79" x 101" (14 x 18 squares)

Create it: More than 50 fabrics were used in this quilt to create 252 6" squares. It was constructed in two vertical pieces, across the width of the silk noil, with no batting. After machine quilting the two sides, they were joined lap-quilt-style and finished with self-binding.

Nathan's Dragons

Made by: Meryl Ann Butler

Finished size: 51" x 73" (8 x 12 squares)

Create it: This larger quilt for my dragon-loving teen grandson started with a 60-degree kaleidoscope medallion center, pieced slightly larger than needed and lightly quilted onto a piece of Hobbs Thermore Ultrathin batting. Then it was trimmed down to match the width of the 16 patch units directly above and below it. The dragon medallion was centered on top of the wrong side of the flannel, then the 16 block units directly above and below it were added with horizontal seams. Columns 1, 2, 7 and 8 were added in the usual manner. Quilting was done in the usual manner, avoiding the central medallion.

Lady Guadalupe

Create an embellished wall hanging from a motif fabric with a story to tell. In the winter of 1531, Lady Guadalupe appeared to Juan Diego and caused roses to bloom in the snow. He gathered them in his cape so he could bring the miracle to the church fathers. When the roses cascaded out, another miracle was revealed: the perfect image of the Lady was imbedded in the cloth. This cape is on display in Mexico City, where each year, 10 million pilgrims honor the mysterious image of the Lady and request their own miracles from her.

Finished size: 19½" x 25"

Create it: The center motif was cut as large as the motif fabric would allow. Then the design was worked out on graph paper based on those measurements. The center motif was pinned to batting and backing, and outline quilted with gold metallic thread. Twenty three-inch squares were cut, including the four light-colored squares fussy cut from the Guadalupe motif fabric. Upper and lower three-square units were sewn, and stitched to the top and bottom of the center motif unit with horizontal seams. Columns 1 and 5 were added in the usual way. Squares were diagonally quilted with gold metallic thread, borders and self-binding completed. The center motif was embellished with assorted hot-fix crystals. Four rose buttons covered corner seams that didn't quite match!

*Used in this project: Virgin of Guadalupe by Alexander Henry (motif fabric); Crazy for Flannels by RJR (backing/binding); Warm Fleece by the Warm Company; Metallic gold Sliver thread by Sulky; EZ Glitz HotFix Swarovski Crystals by OESD; EZ Glitzer Applicator Wand by OESD.

152

A Quilter's Glossary

Acid-Free Tissue Paper: Tissue paper made without the acidic chemicals that destroy fabric fibers.

Appliqué: Small fabric shapes stitched onto a background fabric.

Backing: The back or bottom layer of a quilt.

Backstitch: A stitch taken backwards to reinforce the beginning and end of each seam.

Baste: To temporarily hold two or more pieces of fabric together with long stitches or pins.

Batting: The soft layer in the middle of a "quilt sandwich" between the top layer and the backing. Batting can be made of cotton, polyester, silk, wool or a blend. It is referred to as "wadding" in the U.K. and Australia.

Batting Density: The compactness of the fibers in a batt. A denser batting is heavier, less pliable and stiffer, and is often used in wall hangings. A less dense batting is softer and has a more flexible drape.

Bias: True bias is a line at a 45-degree angle to the selvage.

Binding: A long strip of fabric, usually bias, that covers and finishes a raw edge of a quilt or garment.

Butt: To match edges or folds so they touch.

Casing: A hem or channel through which a rod is slipped, providing a way to hang a wall hanging or quilt.

Chroma: The intensity of a color.

Crossgrain: The threads that run from selvage to selvage.

Echo Quilting: Quilting stitches that follow the outline of the blocks' basic design and are then repeated, like ripples, every ¼" in concentric lines.

Edgestitch: Stitches made very close to the edge or seamline, about 1/16" away.

Even-Feed or Walking Foot: A special machine foot that grips the top fabric and feeds it forward at the same rate as the feed dogs, reducing underlayer creep.

Fat Quarter: A ¼-yd. piece of fabric cut 18" x 22".

Fusible Web: A web-like material that melts when heat and moisture is applied, creating a bond between two fabrics.

Grading: Reducing the bulk of seams by trimming the individual seam allowances at graduating widths.

Grain: The direction threads are woven in a fabric. The lengthwise grain (warp) runs the length of the fabric, parallel to the selvage. Crosswise grain (weft) runs from selvage to selvage.

Hue: The name of a color, such as red or blue-violet.

Interfacing: Woven or nonwoven fabric used to reinforce or stiffen a fabric adding body, strength or shape. Available in fusible and nonfusible styles.

Loft: The thickness or puffiness of a quilt batting generally ranging from ⅛" (low) to 1" (high).

Medallion Quilt: A quilt assembled around a large central motif.

Muslin: A utilitarian off-white woven cotton fabric.

Nap: Pile brushed in one direction such as velvet or corduroy. When the hand is swept over the fabric in one direction, the fabric will feel smoother; in the other direction, the fabric will feel rougher.

Notions: Supplies and tools needed to complete a sewn project, such as thread, seam ripper, etc.

Patchwork: The process of sewing various fabric pieces together.

Pattern Repeat: The distance required for one complete design on the fabric.

Piecing: To stitch two pieces of fabric together to make a larger piece.

Pile: A fabric with a plush feel, such as velvet, corduroy or terrycloth. Its thickness is produced by cut or uncut fabric loops.

Pivot: To rotate the fabric layers while the machine needle is still inserted through them. (Requires lifting the presser foot.)

Preshrink: To treat fabrics before cutting by laundering or steam-pressing to prevent them from shrinking unevenly in the finished product.

Quilting: The process of machine- or hand-stitching to secure all three layers of a quilt together.

Raw Edge: The unfinished or cut edge of a fabric.

Reinforce: To strengthen a section with short machine stitches.

Rip: To remove unwanted stitches or "de-sew." Using a seam ripper, clip the needle thread every fourth or fifth stitch, then pull the bobbin thread out.

Rotary Cutter: A cutting tool with a round cutting blade, used in conjunction with a ruler and a cutting surface called a mat.

Satin Stitch: A very closely stitched zigzag stitch of any width.

Seam Allowance: The measurement of the width between the stitching line and the raw edge of the fabric.

Seamline: Stitching line.

Selvage: The finished edges on each side of a length of fabric.

Stabilizer: Tissue paper, nonwoven or woven materials, or water-soluble materials that are adhered to fabric before stitching to reduce stitching problems, such as puckering, stretching or slippage.

Stitch-in-the-Ditch: Technique of stitching inconspicuously on the right side of a quilt in the well of a seam or next to a seamline, quilting through all layers.

Stitching Line: Seamline.

Strip Piecing: A method of creating yardage by taking long strips of fabric and sewing them together in a sequence. Often, this newly combined material is then cut apart and resewn.

Subcut: A useful term I first heard from my friend, Liz, this refers to secondary cuts, as in "Cut fabric into a 6" x 44" strip and then *subcut* into 6" squares."

Swatch: A small fabric piece.

Topstitch: To stitch on the right side of a quilt or garment as a decorative element.

Trim: To cut away excess fabric.

Value: The lightness or darkness of a color.

Wales: The lengthwise ribs on corduroy or rib knit fabrics.

Warp: Threads parallel to the selvage edge.

Well of the Seam: The seamline on the right side of the fabric.

Some of these definitions are courtesy of Fairfield Processing (www.poly-fil.com/glossary.asp).

Resources

Alexander Henry Fabrics, Inc.
1120 Scott Road
Burbank, CA 91504
818-562-8200
www.ahfabrics.com
Specialty printed cottons, including cowgirl-themed fabrics and
Lady Guadalupe fabrics.

Bali Fabrics
21787 Eighth St. East, Suite 1
Sonoma, CA 95476
800-783-4612
www.balifab.com
Bali batik fabrics, including flannels and Princess Mirah designs.

Benartex
1359 Broadway, Suite 1100
New York, NY 10018
212-840-3250
www.benartex.com
Printed cotton fabrics, including Fossil Fern flannels, Bee Happy
and Caryl Bryer Fallert's Aurora Borealis lines; Minkee Blankee
microfiber plush; and Carol's Zoo lamb kit.

Bernina of America
3702 Prairie Lake Court
Aurora, IL 60504
630-978-2500
www.berninausa.com
Locate your nearest dealer on the Web site to find: Isacord thread;
hot-fix crystals; EZ Glitzer applicator wand, hot-fix crystals and
heavy-duty stand; PolyMesh Cut-Away embroidery stabilizer;
505 Spray and Fix; sewing machines; embroidery machines; and
walking foot.

Blumenthal Lansing Company
1929 Main St.
Lansing, IA 52151
563-538-4211
www.Blumenthallansing.com
Buttons, including LaMode.

Carol's Zoo
992 Coral Ridge Circle
Rodeo, CA 94572
510-245-2020
www.carolszoo.com
14" lamb is one of many two- and three-piece stuffed animal
patterns available.

Cherrywood Fabrics
P.O. Box 486
818 S. Seventh St.
Brainard, MN 56401
888-298-0967
www.cherrywoodfabrics.com
Hand-dyed suede-look cotton fabrics, including Alaska Sunset and
Blue Lagoon gradations; swatch card available.

Clotilde, LLC
P.O. Box 7500
Big Sandy, TX 75755-7500
800-772-2891
www.clotilde.com
Sewing and quilting notions for more than 35 years.

Clover Needlecraft, Inc.
1007 E. Dominguez St., Suite L
Carson, CA 90746
800-233-1703
www.clover-usa.com
Quilting and sewing notions, including chalk markers, mini iron,
deluxe needle-threader, rotary cutters and mats, bodkins and flat
flower head pins.

Coats & Clark
Consumer Services
P.O. Box 12229
Greenville, SC 29612-0229
800-648-1479
www.coatsandclark.com
Thread, including Multicolor Egyptian Cotton machine quilting
thread.

Come Quilt With Me
3903 Ave. I
Brooklyn, NY 11210
718-377-3652
www.comequiltwithme.com
Brooklyn Revolver rotating cutting mat in several sizes and styles; catalog available.

Cranston Print Works
800-876-2756
www.cranstonvillage.com
V.I.P., V.I.P. Select and Quilting Treasures.

Creative Crystal Company
941-377-8027
www.creative-crystal.com
Swarovski Iron-On and hot-fix Austrian crystal rhinestones and BeJeweler Pro hot-fix applicator wand.

Fairfield Processing
P.O. Box 1130
Danbury, CT 06813-1130
800-980-8000
www.poly-fil.com
QuiltCare soap; acid-free tissue paper; cotton quilt gift/storage bags; Machine 60/40 Blend Batting; and pillow forms.

FreeSpirit
1350 Broadway, 21st Floor
New York, New York 10018
www.freespiritfabric.com
Fabrics, including Splash, Freckles, Fundamentals and Estrella flannels.

HTCW Products
800-275-4275
www.htcwproducts.net
HTCW interfacings; available at local fabric stores.

Hobbs Bonded Fibers
200 S. Commerce Drive
Waco, TX 76710
800-433-3357
www.hobbsbondedfibers.com
Thermore® Ultra Thin Batting, Heirloom® Organic Cotton Batting with scrim, and Heirloom 100% Wool batting.

June Tailor
P.O. Box 208
2861 Highway 175
Richfield, WI 53076
800-844-5400
www.junetailor.com
Velvaboard velvet pressing board, Teflon pressing sheet and Fancy Fleece Slotted Ruler; catalog available.

Krause Publications
700 E. State St.
Iola, WI 54990-0001
800-258-0929
www.Krausebooks.com
Publishers of wonderful quilting and sewing books.

Lost Quilt Come Home Page
www.lostquilt.com
A site dedicated to displaying lost and stolen quilts and to providing information on protecting quilts. A page detailing the author's stolen fiber art is at www.lostquilt.com/MerylAnnButler.html

Meryl Ann Butler Studios
www.creativespirit.net/MabArt
www.MerylAnnbutler.com
Artist, quilter, author, educator

Michael Miller Fabrics
118 W. 22nd St.
New York, NY 10011
212-704-0774
www.michaelmillerfabrics.com
Printed cotton fabrics, including glow-in-the-dark Fairy Frost Glow;
Eiffel Tower; and Cuddle Up and Snuggle Up microfiber plush
fabrics.

Moda
13800 Hutton Drive
Dalla, TX 75234
800-527-9447
www.modafabrics.com
Printed cotton and flannel fabrics, including Ruff and Fluff;
available at fabric stores and quilt shops.

Mountain Mist
2551 Crescentville Road
Cincinnati, OH 45241
800-345-7150
www.mountainmistlp.com
White Rose and Cream Rose cotton battings; A Touch of Wool
batting; and A Touch of Silk and A Touch of Cashmere battings
and pillow form.

National Nonwovens
P.O. Box 150
Easthampton, MA 01027
800-333-3469
www.nationalnonwovens.com
Wool/rayon felt; available in fabric stores.

OESD (Oklahoma Embroidery Supply & Design)
12101 N. I-35 Service Road
Oklahoma City, OK 73131
405-359-2741
www.embroideryonline.com
Downloadable embroidery designs, including those in the
Machine-Embroidered Silk Heirloom Baby Quilt.

Olfa North America
33 S. Sixth St.
Terre Haute, IN 47807
800-962-OLFA
www.olfa.com
Mats and cutters, including circle cutter and ergonomically
designed rotary cutters.

P & B Textiles
1580 Gilbreth Road
Burlingame, CA 94010
800-852-2327
www.pbtex.com
Fabrics, including Chroma/Frontier, Stars and Stripes, and a large
selection of tone-on-tones.

Pfaff Sewing Machines
www.pfaffusa.com
Built-in original IDT (Integrated Dual Feed) on many machines.

Prym Consumer USA, Inc.
Attn: Consumer Relations
P.O. Box 5028
Spartanburg, SC 29304
www.dritz.com
Omnigrid and Omnigrip rulers; cutting mats; rotary cutters;
Invisigrip; GlowLine tape; Collins quilting notions; Dritz sewing
notions; Omnigrid scissors; Squizzors; 120" tape measure; flat
flower head pins; and magnetic and wrist pincushions.

Quilters Resource, Inc.
3702 Prairie Lake Court
Aurora, IL 60504
800-676-6543
www.quiltersresource.com
Matilda's Wool batt and wood holder for Clover mini iron.

Robert Kaufman
P.O. Box 59266
Greenmead Station
Los Angeles, CA 90059-0266
800-877-2066
www.robertkaufman.com
Printed cotton fabrics, including Guatemalan Rainbow, and
flannels, including Splish Splash Dots.

RJR Fabrics
2203 Dominguez St., Building K-3
Torrance, CA 90501
800-422-5426
www.rjrfabrics.com
Printed cotton fabrics, including Animal Tales, Kyle's Marketplace
III, Confetti Basics, Crazy for Flannels, Evergreen Inn and Madeline
flannels.

Sterilite Corporation
P.O. Box 524
30 Scales Lane
Townsend, MA 01469
www.sterilite.com
1695 Mini Crate plastic storage box for 6" squares.

Sulky of America
P.O. Box 494129
Port Charlotte, FL 33949-4129
800-874-4115
www.sulky.com
Threads, including Sliver metallic.

Superior Threads
P.O. Box 1672
St. George, UT 84771
800-499-1777
www.superiorthreads.com
Threads, including NiteLite Extra Glow glow-in-the-dark thread and
MonoPoly clear polyester thread.

Susan Deal Design Studio
www.susandealdesigns.com
Designer, author and teacher.

Thai Silks
252 State St.
Los Altos, CA 94022
800-722-7455 or
650-948-8611
www.thaisilks.com
Silks, including noils, dupionnis, brocades, artists' silks and bridal
fabrics; swatches available.

Trish Schmiedl's Threads and Needles
www.TrishsThreadsAndNeedles.com
Machine embroidery designs, including Retro Mola, with no
jumpstitches and machine appliqué designs, including Flamingos.

The Warm Company
954 E. Union St.
Seattle, WA 98122,
800-234-WARM
www.warmcompany.com
Steam-A-Seam 2 and Warm & Natural, Warm Blend, Soft & Black
and Warm Fleece battings.

Weeks Dye Works
1510-103 Mechanical Blvd.
Garner, NC 27529
877-OVERDYE or
919-772-9166
www.weeksdyeworks.com
Specializing in hand over-dyed wools and perle cotton threads.

About the Author

A five-time Bernina/Fairfield Fashion Show designer, Meryl Ann Butler was bitten by the quilt bug in 1982. Her approach to quilting is inspired by her professional art background. She designed the historical First U.S.-Soviet Childrens' Peace Quilt Exchange Project in 1987, which utilized her 90-Minute Quilt techniques. Meryl Ann has taught at major quilt festivals, quilt shops and at various educational institutions around the U.S. since 1986. Her wearable art and fiber art wallhangings are in collections around the world.

With Quilting, The Possibilities Are Endless

Fast-Folded Flower Quilts and Bags
30 Projects for You and Your Home
by Laura Farson

Teaches simple techniques for creating elaborate and beautiful textured flower projects! Using detailed, easy-to-follow instructions and illustrations, readers of all skill levels will create purses, coasters, quilts, wall hangings, and more.

Softcover • 8¼" x 10⅞" • 128 pages
175+ color photos, plus illus.
Item# FFFLD • $21.99

One Stitch™ Quilting: The Basics
20 Fun Projects You Can Finish in a Day
by Donna Dewberry and Cindy Casciato

Create stylish quilt projects in less time with the innovative new quilting method explained in more than 300 step-by-step color photos and illustrations and demonstrated in 20 exciting projects included in this book.

Softcover • 8¼" x 10⅞" • 128 pages
300 color photos and illus.
Item# OSQB • $22.99

Quilting The Complete Guide
by Darlene Zimmerman

Everything you need to know to quilt is in this book, including more than 350 step-by-step color photos demonstrating the quilt making process.

Hardcover • 5⅝" x 7⅝" • 256 pages
350+ color photos and illus.
Item# Z0320 • $29.99

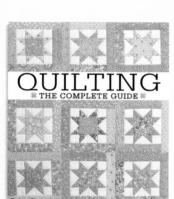

Big Book of Quilting
Hundreds of Tips, Tricks & Techniques
by Krause Publications

More than 625 beautiful color photos and illustrations demonstrate key quilting techniques, and skills such as correctly choosing fabric and thread, and experimenting with quilt template design.

Hardcover • 8¼" x 10⅞" • 512 pages
625+ color photos
Item# 44110 • $24.99

Bundles of Fun
Quilts From Fat Quarters
by Karen Snyder

Perfect for fans of fat-quarter quilts and aspiring quilters alike, this book provides fabric selection advice, instructions for making smaller quilts and adding sashing and borders. Offers variations for 12 coordinating fabrics.

Softcover • 8¼" x 10⅞" • 128 pages
150+ color photos and illus.
Item# FQLQ • $22.99

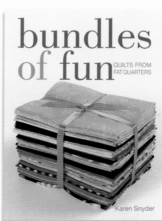